Read! Write!

Explore!

Jeannie Atkins

HOW HIGH
CAN WE CLIMB?

HOW HIGH
CAN WE CLIMB?

THE STORY OF WOMEN EXPLORERS

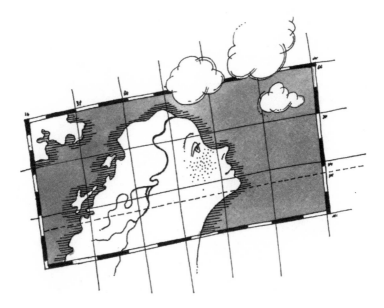

JEANNINE ATKINS
PICTURES BY DUŠAN PETRIČIĆ

Farrar, Straus and Giroux
New York

www.fsgkidsbooks.com

Library of Congress Cataloging-in-Publication Data
Atkins, Jeannine.
    How high can we climb? : the story of women explorers / Jeannine Atkins ; pictures by
Dušan Petričić.— 1st ed.
        p.   cm.
    Summary: Profiles twelve women explorers of the land and sea: Jeanne Baret, Florence
Baker, Annie Smith Peck, Josephine Peary, Arnarulunguaq, Elisabeth Casteret, Nicole
Maxwell, Sylvia Earle, Junko Tabei, Kay Cottee, Sue Hendrickson, and Ann Bancroft.
    ISBN-13: 978-0-374-33503-8
    ISBN-10: 0-374-33503-6
    1. Women explorers—Biography—Juvenile literature. [1. Explorers.   2. Women—
Biography.]   I. Petričić, Dušan, ill.   II. Title.

G200.A84 2005
910'.82—dc22

                                                                    2003056378

To some of the women
who helped me find my path:
Genevieve Bergier Atkins, Margo Culley, Julia Demmin,
Ann Jones, Jean Matlack, and Margaret Quamme
—J.A.

For Zlatko, with whom I shared my boyhood dream
of becoming an explorer
—D.P.

CONTENTS

How Wide Is the World? **JEANNE BARET** — 3

How Far Can a River Flow? **FLORENCE BAKER** — 24

How Can We Climb Where No One Has Gone Before?
ANNIE SMITH PECK — 42

How Far North Can We Go? **JOSEPHINE PEARY** — 56

How Can a Continent Be Crossed? **ARNARULUNGUAQ** — 77

How Deep Is the Earth? **ELISABETH CASTERET** — 97

How Many Secrets Can Be Found in a Forest?
NICOLE MAXWELL — 112

How Deep Can We Dive? **SYLVIA EARLE** — 123

How High Can We Climb? **JUNKO TABEI** — 138

How Far Can We Sail Alone? **KAY COTTEE** — 153

How Can We Find Secrets Under Stone and Sea?
SUE HENDRICKSON — 168

How Can We Reach the Ends of the Earth?
ANN BANCROFT — 177

A Note from the Author — 195

Important Years in Women's Exploration History — 197

Selected Books and Web Sites — 200

Index — 205

HOW HIGH
CAN WE CLIMB?

HOW WIDE IS THE WORLD?
JEANNE BARET

Jeanne Baret dreamed about the things she might do when she was old enough to leave home. She longed to wade in the ocean, which she'd never seen. Maybe she would follow a cloud to see where it disappeared. Maybe she'd wear armor and wave a sword to free France, like Jeanne d'Arc, the saint she'd been named for.

When Jeanne Baret became a young woman of twenty-one, a terrible illness swept through Burgundy in central France. Jeanne stayed healthy, but many villagers, including her mother and father, got sick. Jeanne lugged pails of water to the hearth, added sticks to the fire, cooked broth, and whispered, "Mama, Papa, what else can I do?"

Her parents could barely shake their heads. In spite of Jeanne's care and her prayers, they died.

In 1763, not long after Jeanne buried her parents, her older brother moved his family into the cottage, which was nicer than his nearby home. Jeanne dragged a straw mattress to the attic, where the roof was so low that the herbs she'd hung from the beams brushed her face as she slept. In the morning, she stumbled over shoes left on the stone step by the door. She weeded cabbages and carrots, washed laundry in tin tubs, and cooked pots of soup.

When her brother's wife was busy with her baby, Jeanne tried to amuse the other children by making puppets from old socks and singing silly songs. Holding up the hem of her long dress, she led them through meadows to look for butterflies and frogs. When they got tired, they all plopped down on their backs to find shapes in the clouds. Jeanne told tales about giants, fairies, pirates, and boys with magical boots that let them travel twenty leagues in a single step. She told them how Jeanne d'Arc had led troops of the French Army.

"Didn't they know she was a girl?" her niece asked.

"She wore men's clothes as a disguise," Jeanne said. "Of course, there was trouble when people found out."

"That's a stupid story," her nephew complained. "Tell us about shipwrecks and treasure."

As Jeanne told stories about the sea, she remembered her old hopes of traveling beyond the place where she'd been born. She lay down in the attic, which was hot in summer and cold in winter, and went to sleep to the sounds of the baby crying and of her brother arguing with his wife. She dreamed that a rowboat soared to the roof and swept her far away.

Then a young man started asking her to join him on

moonlit walks. He was kind and had green-brown eyes, but when he talked about a wedding, Jeanne felt as if someone had pushed her into a room and slammed the door. How could she agree to spend the rest of her life in the only village she'd ever known?

One day a peddler told her about a widowed gentleman, Dr. Philibert Commerson, who needed a housekeeper.

"Does he have children?" Jeanne asked.

"One baby, whom he sent to an aunt to raise. I think there's a cat."

Jeanne didn't mind cats. She wanted to go to bed without hearing tears and fights, and maybe wake up without hitting her head on the roof. She packed her few things and hiked past poppy fields until she was offered a ride in a farmer's wagon. She knocked on the doctor's door and asked for the job.

"Won't your parents miss you?" asked Dr. Commerson.

"I'm an orphan, sir. I need to make my own way." Jeanne made a swift sign of the cross to bless her parents' souls, then scratched the cat's ears. "I can wash and iron, bake bread and tarts and—"

"I ask only that you don't touch my collections," Dr. Commerson interrupted. He waved his hand at shelves crowded with old birds' nests, broken eggshells, jars of feathers, bowls of stones, and dried grasses, leaves, and mushrooms.

Jeanne began to work at once. She folded shirts and put them in a wardrobe along with sprigs of lavender from the garden she tended. She polished the doctor's boots and powdered the white wig he wore when he went to Paris to talk with other renowned scientists and professors, for though he

had been trained as a physician, he'd given up practicing
medicine to work as naturalist to the King. He found tramp-
ing through woods and meadows to sketch and study plants
more amusing than mending broken arms and legs.

Dr. Commerson enjoyed the apple tarts Jeanne baked in
fall, the simple soups she made in winter, and the strawber-
ries she served in a cabbage leaf in spring. But after she
had worked for a year, Dr. Commerson told her he'd rather
she leave sheets untucked, pillowcases wrinkled, pots un-
scrubbed, and floors unswept while she helped with his collections. He taught her some Latin so she could label plants,
and he didn't complain when she read books instead of dust-
ing them. He showed her how to place a cut plant on the
smooth wooden surface of a press, cover it with thick paper,
then turn a crank to lower another block that pressed the
plant. When the leaves and stems were flat and dry, Jeanne
carefully lifted them and pasted them in a notebook.

One day she brought in a letter stamped with the King's
seal.

Dr. Commerson tore it open, read quickly, and said, "I've
been invited to join the first French expedition around the
world!" He kissed one of Jeanne's cheeks, then the other, then
both cheeks once again. "We will sail across not only the Atlantic but also the vast Pacific Ocean! It's full of undiscovered
islands. Maybe even a continent!"

Dr. Commerson got busy making plans and spreading
maps across the kitchen table. Jeanne peered over his shoulder as he scribbled beside dotted lines, noting possible shores
to visit. While she mixed pastry batter or sliced a vanilla pod
to dig out its tiny sweet beans, Dr. Commerson told her about

vines that scented the South American air. When she grated a nutmeg, he could hardly contain his excitement about the warm islands where these nuts sprouted on boughs and cinnamon grew as bark on trees.

"Besides discovering new foods or spices, I might find medicinal roots or leaves that can save people's lives," he said.

But as the departure date grew near, he began to worry about storms that stirred waves higher than houses. Like most gentlemen about to set sail on a wooden ship, he wrote his will. He brought the legal parchments to the hearth, where Jeanne was wringing out laundry. "If anything happens to me, will you see that my little boy gets whatever he needs?" he asked.

"Of course," she replied.

"The aunt who cares for him is a good woman, but he'll be old enough for school soon. I want him to have the best education."

"Certainly."

"And you'll make sure the plants, rocks, and animal specimens I collect get to universities?"

"I expect you'll be back to see to that." Jeanne picked up a basket filled with damp linen to haul outside. She was tired of comforting him about a journey she hadn't been asked to join.

As he hurried beside her, his voice turned even gloomier. "The ship might be invaded by pirates. A wind might take us toward islands where wild-eyed men wave spears."

"It's a big, grand ship, you said?" Jeanne clipped a clothespin onto a billowing sheet.

"The biggest and grandest." Dr. Commerson cheered up.

"Two ships will go—one to carry food and supplies and some of the marvels we'll bring back."

"So there will be many sailors?"

"About three hundred crew and officers, I'm told. What with the chance of scurvy and other dread diseases, there will be another doctor or two. An astronomer is coming to study stars in different hemispheres. A geologist will collect stones and—"

Jeanne interrupted. "Won't all those people need someone to cook and clean and sew?"

"Yes. There will be cooks, and carpenters to fix wrecked beams, and sail makers to mend sails torn by the high winds."

Jeanne prayed a few swift, silent words to Jeanne d'Arc, then said, "I want to go!"

Dr. Commerson's mouth fell open. He managed to say, "Women don't sail around the world!"

"Why shouldn't I be the first?"

"Women aren't strong enough, I suppose."

Jeanne kicked aside the laundry basket she'd lugged. It landed in the vegetables. "I'm not the sort to blow away."

"True, but one lady among three hundred sailors might provoke ungentlemanly conduct. Jeanne, I could use someone who knows about collecting and preserving plants. But where would you sleep and change your clothes? I'll leave you salary enough to last the two years or so I'm gone. Someone must look after the cat. And some say I've been selfish, keeping you here with my collections. You'll finally have a chance to meet a young man and start a family."

"I like plants," she said.

"It's not possible for you to go." He sighed. "There's no use in dreaming."

Jeanne supposed there wasn't. She went inside and started packing nets for collecting butterflies and fish. She filled trunks with magnifying glasses, tweezers, droppers, scissors, knives, string, pins, and glass jars and pillboxes for storing seeds. During the following weeks, she packed books with drawings of plants and leather journals with blank pages.

In the fall of 1766, Dr. Commerson was ready to head for the coast of France. He waved his letter from the King, but several stagecoach drivers refused to travel far because of recent robberies on the highways. Finally he found a twelve-year-old lad who said, "Why should I be afraid? I have nothing worth stealing. Any robbers are bound to point their knives at you, sir."

The boy wasn't tactful, but he had two horses and a coach, which he filled with the doctor's trunks. Dr. Commerson took goodbye sniffs of flowers, kissed Jeanne's cheeks, and climbed into the coach. The boy lifted the reins.

"Bon voyage!" Jeanne called.

Clouds of dust rose from the dirt road as the horses galloped off. Jeanne brushed grit from her eye, then looked down at the wide stone step she'd swept a thousand times. Would she sweep it a thousand more times before the ship returned? She thought: *I can stay here and dust, or I can sail around the world. But how can I get aboard the ship?*

Sadly she strolled to the garden and stood ankle-deep in the tangled pumpkin vines and dried bean stalks. The air smelled of grapes turning purple. She closed her eyes and thought of Jeanne d'Arc standing in her garden long ago. No angel swooped or whispered here, but Jeanne thought of how Jeanne d'Arc had dressed in men's clothing to lead an army. Wearing a helmet and armor, a peasant girl could not be distinguished from a gentleman.

Jeanne ran inside, grabbed the sewing shears, and lopped off her hair until it hung just below her ears. She rummaged through the wardrobe to find a pair of old trousers and a shirt she'd shrunk in the wash. She whipped off her apron and dress and put on Dr. Commerson's old clothes. She tucked the shirt deep inside the baggy trousers, which she cinched around her waist with a rope. If she added a jacket or two, she would be able to cover the curves of her chest and hips.

She took the cat to a neighbor, fastened the shutters, bolted the door, and left the house. With only a rucksack for luggage, Jeanne easily found a ride to the harbor. The coach rattled past wild roses and farms where honeybees buzzed around straw hives and goats scrambled over rocks. Finally the stagecoach clattered across cobblestones and stopped by the wharves. The ship was bigger than anything she'd ever seen except the sky.

She learned that one ship had already sailed with Admiral Bougainville. But the *Etoile* had remained, first for repairs, then to wait for a change in tides and more favorable winds. Jeanne made her way through a crowd to find the captain speaking with members of the King's family, mapmakers, well-wishers, and gamblers taking odds on whether any one of them would ever be seen again. Some of the expedition scientists, including Dr. Philibert Commerson, were talking nearby.

"Excuse me, sir," Jeanne addressed the captain, using her deepest voice. "Is there room aboard for a hardworking lad? I could work in the kitchen or be a cabin boy."

"I wager you've never been to sea." The captain frowned as he looked from her smooth bright cheeks to her small hands, roughened from work in the garden. "It looks like you haven't yet begun to shave. How old are you? Do your parents know you want to go to sea?"

"I'm an orphan, sir. I need to make my own way."

Dr. Commerson turned from his conversation to cast a sharp look at Jeanne. She saw she'd have to not only remember to keep her voice deep and gruff but be careful about the words she chose. Dr. Commerson stepped over. His nostrils widened, the way they did when he was trying to place a scent. Jeanne realized her clothes must smell like the lavender she'd always tucked in his wardrobe. Fortunately, the wind stank of old fish.

"The boy is looking for a job," the captain said, then turned to Jeanne. "Your name is?"

"Jean," she replied, drawing out the "ah" sound in the masculine form of her name.

"Well, Jean." Dr. Commerson, too, emphasized the soft "ah" sound. "I could use a cabin boy to help organize my scientific equipment. Once we're ashore, I'll need help carrying my collecting boxes and baskets."

"Thank you, sir!" Her voice started to swerve high with happiness, but she tugged it down as he took another look at her smooth cheeks.

Problems with the ship kept the *Etoile* on land until early in 1767. After it set sail, storms split masts and damaged the hull, so they returned to shore to make repairs. In March, the anchor was raised again. The captain spelled out rules, including those for stowaways. "Any boy not signed on will be tossed to the sharks! Now then, let out the sails!"

As the ship left shore, Dr. Commerson and other gentlemen saluted the French flag. Sailors in checked shirts scrambled up and down the rigging, letting out sails and singing chanteys. Chickens squawked. Cows brought along for milk swayed in the longboats, which were used as pens.

For a few minutes, Jeanne thought she'd made a terrible mistake. She didn't even know how to swim. But she stayed on the deck for hours, while seasick people leaned over the railings or carried basins below deck. *Her* stomach felt queasy, too, but she kept her balance on the lurching deck. She was determined to miss nothing. The ship had seemed huge when she saw it from the wharf, but of course the world was even bigger.

Every evening, one sailor played the fiddle, others danced, and many told stories, often about sweethearts left behind. As the sailors discussed in detail the parts of the body a woman kept hidden, Jeanne retreated to Dr. Commerson's cabin, which smelled of the waxy scent of burnt candles and the camphor and alcohol used for preserving insects. There was always plenty of work, especially after the high waves of a storm made the ship tilt to one side and rearranged the doctor's collections.

As weeks passed, book covers warped and pages puffed in the damp, salty air. Dr. Commerson grew more eager to reach shore. He complained about suppers of salted meat and biscuits so hard that they had to be dipped in weak tea or he'd risk breaking a tooth. "What I'd give for some sweet green grapes!" he said with a sigh.

"Yes, and apples that crunch when you bite into them," Jeanne said.

"I had a housekeeper who made the most exquisite apple tarts," Dr. Commerson said.

"I miss a crusty loaf of bread that's soft in the middle," Jeanne said quickly. "With lots of butter, especially in spring, when it tastes of the buttercups and clover the neighbor's cows ate."

"I had a neighbor with a cow, too"—he studied her with the keen eye he usually reserved for plants—"that grazed on buttercups."

"A lot of cows like buttercups." Jeanne made her voice especially gruff and changed the subject. "I'll be glad to wash my face in water that doesn't sting my eyes with salt."

They had spent more than two months at sea when Jeanne spotted a wren that must have half flown, half blown from shore. They sailed safely into the harbor, which was filled with ships flying Spanish, British, Dutch, Portuguese, and French flags, then anchored at Montevideo, in a river banked with white lilies.

The sailors lugged aboard timber to mend masts and planks that had been broken or beaten in storms. They sailed to Rio de Janeiro, where, in the evenings, they urged Jeanne to join them at dance halls near the wharves. Jeanne was glad that, as Dr. Commerson's able servant, she could instead go along with him, the captain, and other gentlemen to dinners where men talked about gold and emerald mines, sugar plantations, and rubber trees whose sap was shaped into bouncing balls.

Some of the men were homesick, and once Dr. Commerson reminisced about the sad death of his lovely wife and the house he'd left with a loyal maid. "She's as trustworthy as you, Jean." Dr. Commerson slapped Jeanne's shoulder, which was padded with layers of shirts.

During the next two months, while the ship was repaired, Jeanne was happiest when she and Dr. Commerson hiked in the damp green forests, where purple and pink orchids dangled from trees. They were so busy pointing out exotic bushes and trees that there was little time for talk. They hauled plant presses and wicker baskets, and kept an eye out for poisonous ants and snakes and for spiders as big as their hands. They trekked around swamps of wild rice and past sugarcane and pineapple plants. They pried, poked, and shook seeds from the centers of flowers. They found vanilla vines twisting up palm trees, so laden with blossoms that they guessed a thousand flowers might bloom from one vine.

Dr. Commerson picked a slender, curved fruit from a tree, peeled off the yellow skin, and ate the soft, sweet banana. He named a vine with violet blossoms *Bougainvillaea* after the leader of the expedition. "It never hurts to get on the good side of an admiral," he confided to Jeanne.

They explored the coasts of Brazil and Uruguay for almost two months and might have stayed years, but in July 1767 it was time to set sail again. The crew hauled aboard barrels of beans and flour and crates of chickens. They herded cattle onto the ship, hoping they'd have enough to eat once they reached uncharted seas.

They sailed for southernmost South America. Winds and currents were so strong that the ship took four days to enter the Strait of Magellan. Dr. Commerson got seasick, but a few days later he joined sailors in sliding across the deck, which was covered ankle-deep in snow. He and Jeanne sketched penguins and the snowcapped mountains that rose along the shore. More snow fell, and they passed the time in his cabin dissecting fish. When they reached the Pacific Ocean, in January 1768, everyone gathered on deck and sang the Te Deum to celebrate.

They headed north, watching for unmapped islands, or perhaps even a continent no one from Europe had yet seen. At last they arrived at an island with coconut palms and red-and-green birds swooping for fish. There were also twenty naked men waving spears. The Admiral ordered the French ships to keep sailing past islands they called the Dangerous Archipelago in search of friendlier shores.

As the two ships crossed the equator, the air felt steamy. Everyone except Jeanne peeled off jackets, pushed up shirt sleeves, and yanked off boots.

"Aren't you hot?" one sailor asked Jeanne.

"Oh, no," she said, though sweat soaked her bulky clothes. She longed to roll up her trousers but was afraid her slender legs would give away her disguise.

After several more weeks on the Pacific, someone spotted mountaintops on an island. The ships were steered through strong currents around coral reefs. Smiling brown-skinned people rowed toward them in dugout canoes, raising baskets filled with coconuts and mangoes or waving green branches. The sailors waved back wildly at the women, who wore wreaths of flowers instead of shirts.

In April 1768, the anchor was dropped, and all rode the longboats to the shore of the lovely island. They waded through waves that crashed onto black sand. Blue parakeets, green turtledoves, and brown birds with orange beaks flew over palm trees. The explorers learned that the islanders called their home Tahiti, though the Admiral planted a French flag and proclaimed it New Cythera. "Cythera was the island where Aphrodite, goddess of love and beauty, rose from the sea foam," he explained.

He traded nails, beads, buttons, and rolls of red flannel for good things to eat. He ordered the men to make maps, but many, who hadn't gazed upon a woman in months, much less women wearing little but flowers, were distracted. Others played with a silly black-and-white goat that nibbled on their trousers.

The small houses of Tahiti had roofs thatched with dried plants. The scant clothing worn by people was made by pounding fibers from bark. Jeanne and Dr. Commerson grew fond of the coconut, a fruit that was dish, drink, and dessert all in one. They collected many plants and labeled stems, stamens, and seeds.

One day a man from the island peered at Jeanne and shouted something in Tahitian. He waved his hands to show he thought she was a girl.

"No," Dr. Commerson said. "Jean is a boy."

The islander shook his head and playfully lifted her jacket.

Jeanne took a big breath and willed her chest to look more muscular than soft.

Some sailors carrying supplies stopped to take a closer look at her. One scowled and said, "I never saw him shave."

He pulled her jacket from her to reveal arms that were pale, strong—and unmistakably a woman's.

"Jeanne!" Dr. Commerson threw open his arms, then blushed and dropped them by his side. "How did you get here?"

"We've been tricked!" a sailor cried.

"I knew it!" another said. "I always said he never changed his clothes in front of anyone. Nobody listened to me! She's as bad as a stowaway."

"Worse! Feed the liar to the sharks! Somebody get the Admiral. He will punish her."

Admiral Bougainville had already heard the shouting.

"I meant no harm," Jeanne told him.

The Admiral's face wrinkled as he thought. Meanwhile, sailors looked at one another as if trying to guess if anyone else might be disguised. A few rolled their sleeves higher, flexed their biceps, and stroked their beards to make sure others were certain they were male.

Jeanne closed her eyes to pray, but listened to palms swaying on warm breezes. Waves crashed on the sand. Would these be the last sounds she heard? She cried, "Please, sir! I wanted to see the world!"

"Did you know he was a girl?" the Admiral asked Dr. Commerson.

He shook his head. "Perhaps I was a fool."

"Perhaps we were all fools." The Admiral smiled. "Does it matter if a sailor is called Jean or Jeanne? He—pardon me— she may stay."

Jeanne half bowed and half curtsied toward the Admiral, thinking that he hadn't been chosen to lead an expedition because he was easily shocked.

A few days later, everyone waved goodbye to the people of Tahiti, who gave their new friends baskets of fruit and the funny little goat with white whiskers. Jeanne still wore her old shirt and trousers, and most people couldn't break the habit of calling her Jean. A few sailors peeked into Dr. Commerson's cabin to check for signs of a secret romance. They always found him and Jeanne busy labeling tins of seeds or finding space for preserved blossoms and fruits.

The ships passed more islands. Then the wind stopped, and for weeks the voyagers saw nothing but sea. Under the hot sun, the ships rocked slightly on small waves but barely moved forward. The *Etoile* smelled of the melting tar that sealed the planks. The dried beef was long gone, and the barrels with beans were getting low. Finally the lookout spotted a long stretch of waves curling and frothing. "Land!" he cried.

Some hoped this might be an unclaimed island or even an unknown continent. Most would be satisfied with fresh food and water. They sailed closer, but had to turn back because the wide coral reefs near shore could wreck the hull. The Admiral didn't want to take the time to land and use up their meager supplies with no guarantee that they'd find food onshore. No one knew that in June 1768 they were probably the first Europeans to sight the east coast of Australia.

As more weeks passed, they sailed through many storms. Blood rimmed the teeth of men with swollen tongues and blackened gums. Some men coughed or rubbed their swollen feet. Others swayed on weakened legs, which was an even more advanced sign of scurvy, a disease that could be fatal. Sailors often wished they'd stayed ashore, but no matter how many were sick, there was always someone well enough to play the fiddle. There were always at least a few sailors who sang and danced on deck at sunset. And there was always someone able to feed crackers to the little black-and-white goat, letting his hands be tickled by its whiskers.

Jeanne remained healthy, but she began to hate the salty taste of the sea on her lips. She was always thirsty. She tried not to think about the sweet well water back home or the brown-gold crust of long loaves of bread. She grew thin but was much better off than the men, including Dr. Commerson, who was struck with dysentery and a fever that kept him in his narrow cot. Jeanne brought him cups of weak tea, pressed cool cloths on his forehead, and washed his sheets after they became soaked with sweat.

"I'll never see another shore," Dr. Commerson moaned. "Will you make sure my little boy remembers me? And that our collections reach home for scientists to study?"

"You must get better," Jeanne said.

They sailed past South Sea islands, stopping at one where the hunting and fishing were poor, and scorpions, snakes, and even an earthquake prompted them to move on. They sailed past other shores, terrified of stopping, while more of the voyagers got sick. They were so low on food that sailors fought over moldy bread. Some gnawed on leather boots or hunted rats. The butcher wept as he raised a knife above the little goat.

They sailed through the Indian Ocean and finally reached Mauritius, an island east of Africa, to which France had made some claims. At last they got their fill of fresh fruits and meat. They met people with skin colors as varied as the bark of the island's sandalwood, mahogany, and ebony trees. A local healer gave Dr. Commerson tea made from the bark of the taratana tree. Although this lowered his fever, he remained weak from dysentery.

When he felt well enough, he and Jeanne looked for enormous ferns, wild rice, and orchids. They found leaves big enough to use as hats or plates. They heard the chatter and cooing of pelicans, parrots, pigeons, green doves, and birds of paradise. Dr. Commerson often stopped to rest. He drew pictures of baobab trees while Jeanne pressed red lilies between warm, flat stones.

When the ship was ready to depart the big island, Dr. Commerson refused to board.

"We have only to sail around Africa, then past Spain, and we'll be in France," Jeanne said.

"It's still a month or two at sea." He shook his head. "My health won't last even on land."

"You must have hope."

"I'm a doctor. I can't hide my illness from myself. But, Jeanne, you must return to France. You may be the first woman to sail around the world!"

"I won't leave you when you're ill. Other ships from France will stop here. No one says I must end my voyage on the same ship on which it began." If he was going to be stubborn, she'd be stubborn, too. Besides, there was still a lot to discover on this big island. And she preferred sleeping under warm breezes to tending linen that needed to be washed, ironed, and mended.

Jeanne Baret and Dr. Philibert Commerson spent about five years on the island of Mauritius. She was beside him when he died in 1773. Her grief for her friend faded as she fell in love with a French soldier, but her beau died soon after they married. Jeanne's thoughts returned to plants. When a ship from France stopped on the island, she got busy making sure the forty cases of specimens she and Dr. Commerson had collected were carefully loaded; then she climbed aboard. Jeanne Baret returned home, becoming the first woman to sail all the way around the world.

French scientists thanked her for samples of more than three thousand species of plants, seashells, snakeskins, stones, and old teeth, and for the notebooks filled with drawings of plants and animals. Then they sent her on her way.

Jeanne found Dr. Commerson's son and told him about his father's work and death. Of course, the boy didn't remember his father. Jeanne gave the child a packet of old letters curled from the sea air and still slightly scented from the King's sealing wax. He just stared at these, but when Jeanne gave him a sketch his father had made of the little goat from Tahiti, he clutched it to his chest.

Jeanne and the orphaned boy became friends. She took him on hikes and told him tales about magic boots that let wanderers cover twenty leagues in a single step. She told him how Jeanne d'Arc had led an army to save France. She described the wonders of the world.

Before long, Jeanne met a farmer who liked her stories, too. His eyes were the pale brown of newly fallen acorns. They got married in a small stone church. Jeanne found that she liked sowing beans in spring, picking apples in fall, always caring for one small spot of the earth.

In the evenings, she and her husband sat on the stone step to watch their dog chase crickets. Their cat curled in the mint and geraniums. On sunny mornings, Jeanne hung the wash.

As the years went by, neighbors passing the woman at the clothesline forgot that she was the first woman to sail around the world. But Jeanne kept her memories of penguins, palm trees, and wild seas. She never stopped looking at the clouds and thinking of the shores she'd seen.

With every bone in her body, Jeanne Baret knew the width of the world.

—

When Jeanne Baret (1740?–1816), whose name is sometimes spelled Baré or Barret, died, she left her possessions to Philibert Commerson's son. The botanical specimens she collected with Dr. Commerson remain an important part of natural history museums in Europe, including the Linnean Society of London and the Delessert herbarium in Paris. Jeanne Baret was born and died so quietly that no one is sure of the names of the villages where her remarkable life began and ended.

HOW FAR CAN A RIVER FLOW?
FLORENCE BAKER

Florence von Sass looked down at a crowd of men who were shoving, shouting, and eyeing girls they might buy to be white slaves. Most of the people on the platform with Florence were only a few years older or younger than her age of seventeen. As a merchant pushed her to the front of the auction block, Florence recalled the day ten years earlier when her mother had spoken words hard to hear above the sounds of shouts and gunshots. Her mother had tucked a loose strand of hair behind Florence's ear, then pushed her toward the garden. Seven-year-old Florence had hidden as soldiers torched houses, blew up bridges, and chopped down fruit trees. Creeping out of hiding the next morning, she had found the bodies of her mother and father on the floor of her empty house.

There were few places where an orphan could be safe during the 1848 Hungarian revolution. Florence felt lucky that one of her teachers had taken care of her until the teacher married. Then Florence had spent the next few years doing whatever she felt was necessary to survive. She had left the danger and poverty she'd known in Hungary by fleeing to Moldavia, where, along with some girls who stood beside her now, she'd been captured by Turkish slavers. Florence tucked a strand of blond hair behind her ear. She wished she could remember the last words her mother had spoken to her.

A man shoved her from the auction block. Florence stumbled toward a gentleman with shoulder-length hair and a thick brown beard. He said, "Go. You may go."

Florence looked from him to the shorter man beside him, who explained, "My friend bought you only to save you. You're free. You can go home."

She was too stunned to speak. And she didn't have a home.

"I guess the auctioneer lied when he said she spoke English," the shorter man said.

"I must thank you." Florence spoke up. Living on the streets, she had learned some of several languages.

"So you do speak English!" the tall, dark-haired man said. "Then I should introduce myself. I'm Samuel Baker. Would you like supper? You could join my friend and me."

"I am Florence von Sass," she said. "And I am hungry."

Samuel chose a tavern with a view of leafless plum trees and the frozen Danube River. As they ate beef and onions sprinkled with paprika, he and his friend talked about the hunting trip they'd been on before the river froze and they'd stopped here in the Balkans. Samuel told Florence about leaving his daughters in his sister's care after his wife died a few years before. He gazed out the window and said, "I wish I could have saved every girl on those auction blocks."

"Why did you choose me?" Florence asked.

"There was something sad about the way you reached up to push your hair behind your ear," Samuel said. "And something determined in your eyes."

Samuel asked Florence to join him and his friend on their way to Bucharest, where he was to begin work overseeing the building of a railroad. Samuel booked a room for Florence in the inn where they stayed, and they met for meals. Sam, as he asked Florence to call him, spoke to her of his adventures, which included hunting lions and elephants in Africa. By the end of a year, Sam's work had almost been completed, and he and Florence had discussed marriage and other dreams.

One afternoon Sam said, "For at least two thousand years, people have wondered where the Nile River begins. It could be the longest river in the world! Some think the source might be surrounded by snow-covered mountains. Others say the source is a lake so close to the equator that no one could survive the heat there."

"Wouldn't it be wonderful to find out?" Florence said.

"I don't suppose I should have much chance of reaching the Nile's source, when hundreds of men have failed." His eyes glittered above his thick beard. "Of course, I am strong and a good hunter. And I can afford a long trip. But, Florence, my life has changed because of you. If I went, it could be years before I returned. I can't ask you to wait that long to become my wife."

"But I must go with you!" Since meeting Sam, Florence had spent most days perfecting her English, embroidering the sleeves of long dresses, and tidying her rented room. She was grateful to have food on a table and a roof over her head, but she saw now that she missed having a sense of purpose.

"Florence, we'd have to cross deserts and spend months, or more likely years, in deep forests."

"I never liked winter much."

"Most men who go into the jungle never come back." Sam shook his head. "No, I must send you to England, to meet my daughters and enjoy all the elegant things you deserve. You've already waited too long for a chance to live like the lady you are."

"Why shouldn't a lady be an explorer?"

"Darling, I couldn't promise you'd be safe."

"No one can promise that." Florence pushed back a stray lock of hair and remembered the morning she'd found blood and bodies on the parlor floor. "Sam, I'm not ashamed that I washed floors for a living and slept beside potato fields when I couldn't afford a roof. But I'd like to meet your daughters when I have something more to show for myself. Wouldn't it be lovely to say that I explored Africa with you?"

"To tell the truth, I can't quite imagine Africa without you. Perhaps it could be a sort of honeymoon."

Florence and Sam married simply, then left the Balkans to go to Egypt, where they ordered barrels of flour, crates of chickens, drinking water, and beads and red flannel to trade. Florence bought a hair ribbon with red, green, and white stripes, the colors of Hungary's flag. Besides tents and blankets, she packed good china and a silver teapot. Just because they'd be in deserts or jungles didn't mean they shouldn't enjoy a proper cup of tea.

The first part of the Nile voyage wasn't especially daunting. It was a common trip for merchants, missionaries, and even a few tourists. As the Bakers and the sailors and servants they'd hired left Cairo, light from the setting sun glinted on the gold domes of mosques. The sails of the *dahabiah* fluttered. Behind their long, narrow boat, two barges carried camels, horses, and donkeys. The travelers sailed against the river current, which flowed from south to north, and enjoyed long views of pale sand and of the pyramids. At night they stopped to camp and let the animals wander and graze.

After twenty-six days on the Nile, they noticed that the river had narrowed and was beginning to flow faster, between cliffs. Florence and Sam decided to lead a caravan of servants south across the desert, then return to the river at Khartoum, where the two main branches, the White Nile and the Blue Nile, joined to flow north to the sea.

They set out on camels across the hot sand. After one fifteen-hour day riding sidesaddle, Florence hitched up her skirts and rode astride. Balancing was tricky enough when she could grip the camel with her legs, and she wanted to see everything that lay ahead, not just half of the view.

Sometimes so much sand whirled in the wind that the sky turned dark. Even with a veil across her face, Florence felt the sand sting her eyes. Her throat grew dry. But a sip of water from a goatskin was all she needed. And it was worth some discomfort to see gazelles run across brown sand under brilliant blue skies.

The travelers crossed about a thousand miles of the Nubian Desert before reaching Khartoum. They used the city as their base while spending most of a year following tributaries of the Blue Nile, the more easterly branch. Florence, who'd had enough of wearing fashionable but cumbersome long dresses, bought light linen fabric and sewed tunics and trousers for Sam and herself. Sam cut and stitched leather for saddles and packs. They took Arabic lessons. They met English travelers and talked with them about the explorers John Speke and James Grant, who'd been in the middle of Africa so long that most feared they were dead.

In December 1862, Florence and Sam sailed south on the White Nile, which was considered the true Nile—the main branch. The milk-colored river wound past thickets of papyrus and straw houses with rounded roofs. One day Florence heard paddle wheels churn. The steamboat coming toward them was flying the flag of the Netherlands.

Sails were lowered, anchors were dropped, and greetings were exchanged with Alexandrine Tinné, a Dutch explorer. Sam looked relieved to learn that Alexandrine had failed to find the source of the Nile. He didn't begrudge anyone a discovery, but he would prefer to be the one rewarded with medals, money, and opportunities for more exploration.

"I'm afraid we had to turn around," Alexandrine said. Her face was freckled beneath her bonnet. "The river is clogged with dead weeds farther south. We're going to return the boat, get more supplies, and try an overland route."

"Into the mountains?" Florence turned to Alexandrine's mother. "Are you going, too?"

"Of course." Wrinkles spread from Madame Tinné's eyes as she smiled. "I never thought I'd find myself riding camels or sleeping in tents at my age. But if I wanted my daughter's company, I knew I'd have to come with her. She's not the type to stay home."

"All my relatives say it's bad enough that I'm exploring Africa, but unforgivable that I brought Mother along," Alexandrine said.

"As if you could keep me away," her mother said. "Your brothers just want me to take care of the grandchildren."

A sailor pointed to the setting sun. Everyone wanted to sail farther before finding a place to camp for the night.

Sam and Florence waved handkerchiefs until the boat commanded by Alexandrine Tinné was out of sight. Then, as the blue of the sky deepened, and turned pink as the sun moved toward the horizon, the sailors steered to shore and herded the animals off the barges. Cooks rolled out flour barrels, lit fires, and baked flat bread. While night fell, the crew sang and played drums. Florence embroidered napkins by the light of the moon and of lanterns. Sam sketched tamarind and mimosa trees, whose scents sweetened the hot air.

During the following weeks, the air turned more humid. As Alexandrine Tinné had warned, so much dead grass had fallen into the river that it had become too clogged to sail. Sailors climbed out of the boat to hack a path between the reeds and rushes. Some pushed the *dahabiah* while others walked ahead, hauling it with hooks.

In February 1863, they reached Gondokora, which was nearly a thousand miles from Khartoum. Few people sailed south of this city, scented by old lime and lemon groves, which was known for its trade in slaves and ivory. Florence hated the city, and they were getting ready to leave when they met John Speke and James Grant. The British explorers were thin and exhausted but alive. John Speke spoke of the lake he'd discovered on an earlier expedition and had named Lake Victoria after the British Queen. He and James Grant had spent much of the past two years exploring the region around that lake in an effort to prove it was one of the Nile River's main sources. Sam congratulated them with rather forced enthusiasm. He looked happier when John Speke said, "There may be another source besides this lake. We were so low on food that we couldn't explore a river flowing from Lake Victoria. You must go on." Speke showed the Bakers maps he and Grant had drawn, and Sam gave the men his boat.

In March, Florence and Sam headed south into the swampy Sudd, which in the rainy season covered an area the size of England. Some sailors now worked as porters, carrying the luggage, while mosquitoes buzzed around their necks and elbows.

The Bakers also hired people they met along the way to help them transport food and tents. Young couples were often eager for this work, and they left their children, cattle, and fields in the care of relatives for a while. Florence noted that the women, who were the chief farmers in the region, had strong arms and backs from hauling tools or baskets of grain, often while carrying children, too.

They all made their way past papyrus reeds and rotting grasses that hid crocodiles. One camel toppled over onto a woman, who managed to squirm out unharmed. Other camels balked on the edges of marshes and were sold. The donkeys died after being bitten by tsetse flies.

Florence and Sam forged ahead, now mostly on foot. During the following weeks and months, they ran out of plum pudding, biscuits, and tea, but when they stopped for the night, Florence insisted that they spread their Persian carpet in their tent, boil a little water, and put a pretty cloth over a stone or tree stump. Hyenas howled. Florence listened for lions.

One evening an elephant ran through the camp, stepped on a man, and broke his legs. Sam made splints from branches, while Florence ripped cloth to make bandages, which she soaked in sap from mimosa trees and wrapped around his legs. The sap stiffened as it dried to make a cast. The man was carried on a bed they rigged on a camel until he recovered.

The expedition reached a Latuka village where people lived in bell-shaped houses with thatched roofs. The women's dark faces were tattooed, and their pierced lower lips were studded with crystals. They walked a mile every day to fetch water and tended hens in the village. The men wore their hair elaborately twined, braided, and woven with cowrie shells. They hunted ducks and geese and every night set campfires in the fields to keep flies away from their herds of cattle.

Florence and Sam traded buttons, mirrors, copper bracelets, coral beads, and knives for chickens and eggs. "Have you heard of a big lake?" they asked. "A long river?" Some people laughed or shrugged. Others pointed in a direction that seemed likely.

As the expedition got closer to the equator, rain fell more often. Some porters and guides returned to their homes, and Sam and Florence hired new ones willing to travel for a while. They hacked paths through shrubs that got thicker and thornier. The hills became rockier and higher. Malaria made everyone weak, and some people died. Unable to carry everything, the Bakers gave away china teacups and barrels of flour and rice.

Florence's tongue became so dry from thirst and hunger that she could hardly swallow. Her head often ached. When Sam came down with a terrible fever, they set up camp for a few weeks. Florence cared for him until he was well enough to walk again. "Should we turn back?" he asked.

"What would your Queen think if we were to turn around now?" she said.

They trudged on to a village where people grew sesame and hunted antelope. They met a woman named Bacita, who'd been captured by Arabs to be a slave and learned their language before escaping. Ever since they'd left Egypt, Florence and Sam hadn't been able to make much use of the Arabic they'd learned, so they were glad when Bacita agreed to go with them and translate the local language. She helped lead them to the ancient kingdom of Bunyoro, where dome-shaped houses were made of mud and grass. Women steamed fish wrapped in banana leaves. They made black-glazed pottery and ground corn between stones. Their pretty pale brown robes were sewn from fabric made from the bark of fig trees, which had been soaked in water, then beaten.

After a few weeks in Bunyoro, Florence and Sam were told they could meet the King and formally ask permission to see the lake. Florence exchanged her linen tunic and trousers for a dress. She tied her favorite yellow scarf over her blond hair. Sam combed his long hair.

At a tree so large that it could shade almost everyone in

the village, King Kamrasi sat on a copper throne. He wore a cape made from leopard skin.

Sam bowed to the King. Then he explained that they wanted guides to lead them to the great lake.

"You only want to look at the lake?" King Kamrasi asked. "You won't try to steal it or make a home there?"

"No. We just want to make a map," Sam said. "Then we'll leave."

Bacita translated the King's next question. "Why do you bring so many guns?"

"We'll hunt if we can," Sam said. "And we may need to protect ourselves."

"We've brought gifts," Florence said. She and Sam spread out a Persian carpet, a silk shawl, a pair of red shoes, a double-barreled gun, and ammunition. Florence unwound her yellow scarf, fringed with silver bangles, and handed it to the King. Sam offered him his favorite sword. In return, Kamrasi gave them cows and barrels of cider made from the plantains' delicious yellow pulp. He granted the explorers permission to go to the lake, guided by four local women and six men.

The small expedition set out beneath branches so thick that even the air seemed green. They met people carrying jars of salt; they said the salt came from a place where "the water goes as far as eyes can see. You can hold a jar by the shore and water comes to fill it up, then sweeps away."

Florence was heartened by the description of waves. She suffered from headaches but never complained. Then one afternoon, while crossing a swamp on matted plants, she clenched her teeth, tightened her hands, and fell.

Sam rushed over before she could sink into the swamp. He carried her to firm ground, touched her forehead, and realized she was suffering from sunstroke or a bad fever. He spent the next few days sitting beside her, pressing damp cloths on her forehead, and murmuring about the home they'd make in London someday. Florence only moaned in reply.

When it had been a week since she could sit up or eat, Sam lost hope that she would ever get well. He ordered porters to make a litter from canvas and poles to carry her through the forest with them. Each evening when Sam found a place to camp, he looked for a soft patch of dirt where his wife might be buried. One night when she seemed to be barely breathing, he ordered axes to be sharpened and trees cut to make a coffin.

Florence's feverish dreams broke as she heard an ax strike stone. A shovel slammed into dirt. Her mind wouldn't focus entirely, but she thought that she was only twenty-two years old, hadn't yet seen what she'd come for, and wasn't ready to die. With great effort, she opened her eyes.

The next day she sipped a spoonful of soup. She still needed to be carried on a litter the next week, but each day she walked a little on her own, until she could manage to amble on aching, unsteady legs. Finally she was able to hike through the high yellow grasses with Sam.

One day they met a woman carrying jugs of water. "Parkani," she said in response to a question from Bacita.

"She says it is very close," Bacita said. "I think we might reach the lake tomorrow!"

Sam practiced a little speech and instructed the men and women from Bunyoro to salute when he raised the British flag at the source of the Nile. Florence daydreamed about the elegant dress she might wear when Queen Victoria thanked them for their trouble.

The morning of March 14, 1864, she wound around her hair a ribbon with the red, white, and green of Hungary's flag. The exhausted explorers climbed a hill. When they reached the top, they looked down at a lake. The water was so blue and vast that it seemed to belong more to the sky than to the earth. Sam dropped to his knees. He must have forgotten his speech and flag.

Florence's knees buckled. "Go ahead," she said. "I need to rest."

Sam studied her with worried eyes, but when he looked back down the steep rocks, he couldn't help smiling. "I think the lake is only a mile or two away from the bottom of the cliffs. We can reach it and get back here by nightfall."

"I'll stay with Florence," Bacita offered.

The others started to slide and scramble down the rocks. Florence looked at distant blue mountains that rose toward the clouds. A yellow savanna spread north of the lake. She heard a voice that didn't rise quite from inside her but didn't seem to come from outside either. *I'm proud of you.*

Florence knew those were the last words her mother had spoken. She tucked a loose strand of hair behind her ear, lifted her arms, and called, "Wait! We're coming with you." She took Bacita's hand, then let it go as she crouched to set her foot carefully between jagged rocks. They made it to the bottom of the cliffs, then crossed a meadow. Florence could smell moss and cool water.

At last they reached one of the sources of the Nile River, where an elephant dipped its trunk. This was not only a lake but the end of an almost four-thousand-mile journey. Flor-

ence tugged the striped ribbon from her hair and tied it to a branch. She never gave much thought to the land where she'd been born, but she wanted to show how far she'd come.

Sam raced into the water. Knee-deep in waves, he cupped his hands and took a long, long drink. His lips puckered. "It's salty." He laughed, then threw out his arms. Cranes waded through waves that splashed on white pebbles. The air rang with the cries, chirps, chatter, and coos of white egrets, spoonbills, ibis, orange-and-turquoise sunbirds, kingfishers, swallows, starlings, and nightingales. Cormorants spread their black wings to dry. Birds had flown from all over Africa to the water.

"The people nearby call this the Luta Nzige," Bacita said. "Meaning the great water that stopped the locusts."

"It needs an English name." Sam's smile disappeared. "Unfortunately, Mr. Speke and Mr. Grant already named their lake after Queen Victoria."

"We must name this in memory of her dear husband," Florence suggested. "Won't the Queen like that even more?"

"Of course! We'll call it Lake Albert."

That night they pitched tents and planned the trip home, via different tributaries and trails. Florence and Sam bought two dugout canoes from people who lived nearby and set out with their guides toward the northern point of the lake. Each night they camped on sandy beaches and caught fish for supper. In fourteen days, they reached the northern shore.

Then they paddled down a stream they believed was part of the Nile River. The current grew stronger and wilder as the river narrowed between rocks. The guides steered the canoes to shore.

Everyone climbed out and walked beside the river to the bottom of a 130-foot-high waterfall. Sam named the cascade Murchison Falls in honor of Sir Roderick Murchison, who headed the Royal Geographical Society. The porters carried the canoes to the bottom of the waterfall; then everyone climbed back in to ride into the frothing water under the falls. Sam balanced his sketchbook on his knees and, while he drew, murmured, "Hold the boat steady."

They managed to keep the canoe balanced until a hippopotamus appeared, opened its enormous mouth, and dived beneath the boat. Florence grabbed the sides of the canoe as it rose from the water, then crashed back down. Crocodiles raised their heads. Florence counted them in an effort to stay calm. She'd counted fourteen crocodiles by the time the hippopotamus swam away.

The small expedition continued on the river until it became swampy; then they struck out through the forest. They got lost in a bamboo thicket. Their food was low and the hunting was bad, so they made porridge from moldy flour and scraped honey out of trees. They boiled river water with wild thyme for drinking. Often they were so weak that they could barely walk, but every evening Sam drew marshes, mountains, or yellow-breasted pigeons nesting in tamarind trees. He wrote the names of villages and forests on maps. He asked Bacita to make sure their new map of Africa got back to England if he and Florence died.

But they survived, and after months in the forests found their way back to the Nile River. They returned to Egypt, then arranged passage on a ship to England. Friends and family were delighted to see Sam, who many assumed had died years before. Some had never heard of his courageous young wife.

Florence joined Sam at many balls and banquets, but sometimes she stayed home with his daughters. After all, the girls had to get used to their new stepmother.

One night Florence was showing them how to iron a tablecloth without burning their fingers when Sam burst in with the news that he would be knighted for the discovery of Lake Albert. "I'll be called Sir Samuel Baker now!"

Florence threw down the tablecloth and hugged him.

He stepped back from her arms. "There's one problem. I heard that Queen Victoria won't have you in the palace. She says a woman who'd trek through the jungle wearing trousers and whatnot could hardly be proper company." His face clouded, and his neck grew red. "She disapproves of how we met and thinks it's scandalous that we didn't get married in a proper British church."

Florence blushed, too. She picked up the tablecloth she'd tossed down. It snapped as she folded it.

"Mama, what's wrong?" the youngest girl said.

"Nothing, dear." Florence spread the cloth over the table. "Let's make some tea and biscuits and have a party of our own."

A week later, Florence went to the Royal Geographical Society's grand hall. The Queen hadn't come for this occasion, but Florence didn't care. She took a seat in the front row to watch Sam receive a gold medal.

Sam praised the explorers John Speke and James Grant for finding a route to Lake Victoria. He thanked the Royal Geographical Society for its interest in their quests. "And there is one I must thank, one who, though young and tender, has the heart of a lion, and without whose devotion and courage I would not be alive to address you tonight."

Sam left the stage to join Florence. She stood and linked her arm through his. They walked to the podium, where Sam said, "Allow me to present my wife."

The crowd cheered.

—

The question of where the Nile River began would provoke debates and even duels for years, until more explorations proved that the Nile's main sources were Lake Victoria and Lake Albert, which is now sometimes called Lake Mobutu Sese Seko. African exploration continued. Alexandrine Tinné (1835–1869) became the first European woman to attempt to cross the Sahara Desert, where she was murdered.

In 1869, Samuel Baker was hired to help spread Egyptian rule to southern countries and stop the trade in slaves. Once again Florence von Sass Baker (1841–1916) joined her husband on Africa's longest river.

After four years marked by danger, and mostly unsuccessful in their mission, the Bakers returned to England. They traveled to parts of Europe and Asia, but when Sam was offered another job in Africa, Florence said that seven years there had been enough. Sam would not go without her.

HOW CAN WE CLIMB WHERE NO ONE HAS GONE BEFORE?
ANNIE SMITH PECK

One older brother might have been all right, Annie Smith Peck thought. Maybe even two. But three bossy older brothers meant someone was always shooing Annie down from trees, banning her from ball fields, or throwing pillows to keep her off a favorite chair.

At least life with three brothers sharpened Annie's skill at argument. This came in handy at school in the 1860s, when only boys could take certain classes. Why shouldn't a Rhode Island girl who won spelling bees and speech contests learn any language she pleased? Annie fought to study Greek and Latin, which were reserved for boys who might go to college.

She learned several languages, trained as a teacher, and

then taught high school. Annie was twenty-four before she got a chance to enroll at the University of Michigan, which had just started accepting women students. She did so well in her Latin and Greek classes that she was hired to teach classical languages at Purdue University.

Annie was admired by faculty and students, but when she visited her family on holidays, all her mother wanted to know was whether she'd met a suitable young man.

"An intelligent woman has more on her mind than a husband," Annie replied. She had much to be proud of, but when one of her students asked if she'd ever visited Rome or Athens, she didn't confide that she felt something was missing.

She began to put aside a sum from every paycheck. When she reached the age of thirty-three—by which time her mother had stopped asking if she'd ever marry and have children—Annie and a few friends sailed to Europe. Annie admired ancient fountains and broken marble temples. Still, she didn't feel the thrill she'd expected until she boarded a train that ran near the Alps. If the gods and goddesses of the ancients dwelled anywhere, Annie thought, it was on top of these snow-covered mountains rather than amid the crumbling stones of Rome.

Annie sailed to Massachusetts, where in 1886 she got a job teaching Latin at Smith College. But her memory of the Alps didn't fade. She wanted to go back and climb to the peaks.

"Why don't you stick to mountains in New England?" a friend asked. She knew that on vacations, Annie hiked in New Hampshire's White Mountains.

"They're not high enough," Annie said. She considered them a practice ground.

"You could get killed in the Alps," her friend said.

"That isn't my intent." Annie knew that the higher a mountain, the more possibilities there were of being buried by an avalanche or caught in severe and sudden storms. But it seemed foolish to think one could know a mountain's secrets just by looking at it. Mountains were meant to be climbed.

"Aren't you a bit too old to be scrambling up ice and rock?"

"Not yet," Annie said.

When she'd saved some money, she resigned from her teaching job and headed back to Europe, this time with picks, ropes, sturdy shoes, and a few pairs of woolen trousers. In 1895, she became one of the first women to reach the peak of the Matterhorn in the Alps. She stood higher than any of her brothers had ever dreamed of climbing, but there was more to her joy than that. As Annie turned to face the east, south, west, and north, nothing stood in her way.

She returned to the United States and spoke about her adventures at the National Geographic Society in Washington, D.C., where there wasn't even standing room in the crowded auditorium. Newspaper accounts usually emphasized the trousers she'd worn more than the peaks she'd climbed, but Annie filled lecture halls in Boston thirteen times.

Public speaking allowed Annie to earn money to climb some of North America's highest mountains. In 1897, she summited Orizaba, in Mexico, which at more than eighteen thousand feet was the highest point a woman had yet climbed. That wasn't high enough. Annie studied maps and

charts. Although she'd have to climb the mountain to measure it, she believed Mount Huascarán might be the highest
peak not only in Peru but also in all of North or South America.

She found some scientists willing to loan equipment to
gauge the mountain's height, but she needed money to sail to
Peru and pay salaries to guides. She approached companies
whose products she might use: manufacturers of hand cream,
shoes, and chocolate.

"Think of the publicity you'll get when my picture is in all
the newspapers," Annie said.

"Think of what people will say if we help a nice lady tumble off a mountain. No, thank you. Please stay home."

"My trunk is my home," Annie replied.

She couldn't find a sponsor. In 1903, she resigned herself
to debt and sailed from New York to Central America, took a
train across Panama, then sailed south along the coast of
Peru. She spent days on horseback riding narrow paths above
river valleys and black canyon cliffs to Yungay, a village near
the base of Mount Huascarán. She gasped when she saw the
two snow-covered peaks. To get a closer look, she took out
binoculars. Now she understood why no one had ever
climbed the mountain. But she had come too far to turn
back.

The Vinatéa sisters welcomed Annie into their home.
"Don't go," they said. "You are a nice woman. We fear you
won't come back alive." Once they realized she was determined to climb the northern peak, they and other villagers
argued about which way she should go. Some thought the
eastern slope would be impossibly icy. Its glaciers were rid-

dled with crevasses, or deep cracks, which she'd have to go around or cross. Others argued that the western side was even more dangerous, for afternoon sunlight melted snow and caused avalanches.

"Great mounds of snow tumble faster than anyone can run," one villager warned. "They crash like thunder. We hear it way down here."

Annie decided to head up the eastern side, since everyone agreed that the canyons she'd pass on the way were beautiful. "I need people to help me carry food, blankets, and a tent," she said. "I can pay a decent wage."

Many of the Quechua Indians she approached had been converted by Spanish missionaries to Roman Catholicism, but they remained influenced by their ancestors' religion and warned Annie about the dangerous spirits of the forest. "Those who disturb the gods in the mountain will turn to stone," they said. Six men said they would go along if they could carry a wooden cross and a Peruvian flag.

Annie agreed, then explained mountaineering procedures. "We'll tie ourselves together when we climb the steepest peaks. If one of us slips, the others will hold the rope to keep him from falling off a cliff or into a crevasse." So that no one could imagine one falling person dragging along the others, Annie kept talking. "If we make it to the top, it's climbing tradition that, as expedition leader, I will set foot on the peak first."

The six men shrugged and nodded.

"Bring as many ponchos as you can get your hands on." Annie glanced at their bare feet and said, "Borrow heavy shoes from the miners."

Once everyone was ready, they rode horses past adobe houses, silver and coal mines, and a four-mile-long gorge. A stream ran between poplar, willow, and peach trees. When the trail grew steeper, one man stayed with the horses. The others walked ahead with ropes, picks, ice axes, extra clothes, food, pots, a kerosene stove, sleeping bags, a tent, cameras, film, and equipment to measure the mountain.

Eventually the flowers, including yellow broom, blue lark-spur, and cream-colored everlasting, became sparse. Narrow trails ended in rock and ice, where nothing grew. Annie and the men camped, then spent the next day climbing steep and snowy peaks. When they reached a flat place with room for a tent, they decided to camp for the night and try to reach the summit in the morning.

Two men set up the tent and banked snow around it to keep it warm and steady. Annie made observations with a hypsometer, which would test when water boiled and thereby determine the height above sea level. She used a barometer to measure air pressure, which becomes lower as one climbs higher. One man watched over the small kerosene stove. At their current altitude, it took two hours to melt enough snow to make pea soup and cocoa. The others got ready for the next morning's climb by pounding nails into the soles of their shoes to help them stick to the ice.

As everyone ate supper, the men grumbled: What kind of creatures might come here at night? What if it started to snow? Would they freeze during the night? What if someone rolled off the mountain in his sleep? They blew on their cold hands and one asked, "Do you think we're turning to stone?"

"Everything's fine," Annie assured him. "We're almost

there." She didn't point out that the icy top was the most dangerous part of the climb.

Wearing three suits of woolen underwear, two pairs of stockings, vicuña fur socks, and high-laced boots, Annie snuggled into her sleeping bag. Snow blew through folds in the tent, but Annie probably wouldn't have slept much even if she were warm. She couldn't wait until the first beams of sunlight meant she could leave the tent and start the final climb.

Just before sunrise, she pulled on jackets over jackets and mittens over mittens. She wound a nun's veil around her head to keep her face from getting sunburned, and grabbed the smoked glasses that would protect her eyes from the sun's intense glare on the white snow. As she started up, she took two or three long breaths with every step. Then, while slowly lifting a foot that felt heavy, she heard someone shout, "Avalanche!"

Snow plummeted. Rocks and slabs of ice whipped by the climbers' heads. Sliding snow rumbled to a stop in a huge pile just a few steps away from the climbers' toes. Annie's companions started packing.

"We're all right!" Annie said, but no one listened.

"I wouldn't go back up there for all the money in the world," one man muttered as everyone headed down.

Five days later, Annie led four new helpers up the mountain's other side. Some people thought the danger of avalanches was even worse on the western side, but Annie decided to risk it. Near the top, the climbers bound themselves together with ropes. They slammed axes into the ice and hauled themselves upward. Annie scouted paths between the maze of deep cracks in the glacier.

Things went all right until one man's hat flew off and landed in a crevasse so deep that they couldn't see the bottom. Then it began to snow. Annie urged everyone onward and offered salary bonuses, but as snow fell more heavily, the men argued that it was time to pitch the tent and wait out the storm.

They huddled inside while the canvas flapped in the cold wind. All through the night, the men murmured that the spirit of the mountain was telling them to turn around. And as soon as the sun rose the next morning, they started back down. Annie was disappointed, but she agreed that they should leave. The snow was so thick that it covered holes or cracks in the ice, and they walked with extreme caution.

Annie saw failure only as a reason to try again, but snowstorm after snowstorm kept her off the mountain. She waited out the winter, then tried again in May, when the sun was in the north and there might be less chance of avalanches. Annie led a new team almost to the top, where crevasses blocked every possible route to the summit. They had to turn around.

Annie returned to the United States to raise funds by lecturing about her adventures. She visited the White House, where President Teddy Roosevelt praised her efforts but couldn't offer much practical help. She took a train to New York and marched into the office of *Harper's Monthly Magazine*.

"I didn't reach the peak of Huascarán, but I climbed nineteen thousand feet," Annie told the editor. "That's higher than any man or woman now living in the United States has climbed. Next time I mean to get all the way. I believe that's a story your readers will want to hear."

The editor pushed a contract across his cluttered desk. The next day Annie came back for a paycheck. She sailed south two days later.

She tried again, and failed again. While waiting for a change in the weather, she explored the Andes mountain range and hiked along the Amazon River.

A few years passed before the glacier seemed sufficiently covered with snow for Annie to try again. Annie, who was now fifty-six, and four Indian helpers climbed close to the top, where they found a place to camp, then drank cocoa and ate pease meal and toasted maize and, in the morning, Grape-Nuts. They were climbing again at a steady pace when a helper accidentally dropped a knapsack into a crevasse. They couldn't survive long without the stove now at the bottom of the crevasse, since if they couldn't melt snow, they'd have nothing to drink. They returned to the valley, got a new kerosene stove, and set out again.

They'd made it almost to the top when the clouds turned black. It began to snow so thickly that Annie couldn't see the surface a step ahead. Once again, she agreed it was time to turn around.

People in the village near the mountain base said, "Señora, please, don't go back up! Stay here and share our houses! You can be a grandmother to our children!"

Annie had to wonder if she was crazy to risk leaving behind friends who wanted her to live with them like family. But she couldn't look at the mountain without wondering how it would feel to stand on top.

In 1908, she sent for two Swiss mountain guides named Rudolf and Gabriel. The three of them climbed the mountain

with two Indians who helped carry supplies. Domingo and Anacreo stayed in the tent near the top, while Annie and the Swiss guides strapped climbing irons over their boots and tied themselves together with a rope. Cautiously they made their way up the glass-smooth glacial ice. The winds were extremely cold, so Annie secured the rope and asked Rudolf to give her the fur mittens she'd put in his knapsack. After taking them out, he dropped one mitten, which a strong wind blew away. Annie was annoyed, but she simply put two wool mittens on her left hand and wore the fur mitten on her right hand.

They put down their ice axes and stopped to eat, but she was too tired to chew the meat, which had frozen. She just let chocolate melt in her mouth.

The wind got colder and stronger. Annie wiggled her left hand, which was numb. She peeled off the two wool mittens and rubbed her hand with snow until it ached, a sign that the danger of frostbite had lessened. She tugged her wool poncho down over her hand. This made movement awkward, especially when the poncho whipped in the wind, but her hand warmed up.

After seven hours of climbing, the summit was finally within reach. Annie longed to stand on the top, but after years of effort she made herself spend a few minutes to set up the hypsometer to take measurements. Gabriel helped by striking match after match, but winds kept blowing them out. Annie tried to shield the flame from the cold gales with part of her poncho while keeping its other end wrapped around her hand.

"Rudolf!" she called. She hoped that if he held down her

poncho, they might be able to make the flame last long enough to get the instrument to work. Rudolf didn't answer. *Where is he?* she wondered, while once again trying to light the flame and calculating how long it would take to climb to the peak and return to the tent before dark.

When they'd used up twenty matches, Annie gave up hope of measuring the mountain. As she and Gabriel packed the instrument, Rudolf appeared.

"I got to the top!" he shouted.

Annie's mouth fell open. Every word she thought of saying was one a polite lady didn't use.

"Don't worry," Rudolf said. "You planned and paid for the trip. It will be your name that gets recorded. It doesn't matter that I ran ahead."

Ever since Annie had set her heart on this mountain, she'd wanted to be the first person to stand on the top. But the air was so thin that just breathing was an effort. There was no oxygen to spare for words or anger. Annie picked up her ice ax and climbed to the peak.

Look at me now, she wished she could tell her brothers, though it had been decades since they'd tried to stop her from doing anything. She looked down at what mattered more: forests no one had seen from above and the village where her worried friends would be happy to see her whether or not she'd reached the peak. But there was no time for reverie. There was little point in being here unless she could get back. To do that, she couldn't waste a second of the fleeting sunlight.

Annie, Rudolf, and Gabriel roped themselves together. At one point, Rudolf bent to tighten his boot, took off a mitten, fumbled it, and watched it blow away. Annie shook her head in disgust when he admitted he hadn't brought extra mittens. As they went down, he kept switching his mitten from one hand to the other.

"My feet are cold," Rudolf said, not for the first time.

"How are your hands?" Annie glanced at the sun, which had almost disappeared.

Rudolf grimaced.

"Maybe we should dig a cave in the snow and spend the night," she suggested.

"No," Rudolf and Gabriel both said.

Annie nodded.

They continued taking small, probing steps, hoping the snow and darkness didn't hide a crevasse. When the terrain became less steep, they unfastened the line that held them together. Annie sat on an icy slope and slid. It wasn't very professional, but it was fun, at least until she picked up too much speed and bumped over snow and ice. She had to swing open her legs, dig in her heels, and slam down her fists to stop herself before she came to the edge of a cliff. They all made it to the tent, where the two Indians were sleeping. By that time, the fingers of Rudolf's left hand had turned black with frostbite.

As soon as it was light, everyone headed down the mountain. Annie was warmly welcomed by her friends in the village. They found a doctor whose quick actions saved Rudolf's feet, but his left hand had to be amputated. His loss cast a shadow on Annie's victory, but she was still proud when the President of Peru awarded her a gold medal and when, in 1927, the Lima Geographical Society named Mount Huascarán's northern peak "Cumbre Ana Peck" in her honor. She had fought her way to a view she would never forget.

—

Annie Smith Peck (1850–1935) kept climbing. When several students from Yale University challenged her to race them up Nevado Coropuna, one of South America's highest peaks, sixty-one-year-old Annie reached the top in plenty of time to plant a yellow banner emblazoned with VOTES FOR WOMEN *to greet the young men. Then, in her eighties, she returned to the mountains of New Hampshire, ending her climbing career where it had begun. In 1934, the Society of Woman Geographers celebrated her eighty-fourth birthday by giving her a cake shaped and frosted to look like a snow-covered mountain. It was delicious. Annie died the following year.*

Later triangulations of Mount Huascarán showed that it measured about twenty-two thousand feet, which was slightly less than Annie's estimate. It was the highest peak in Peru, though not the highest mountain in South America.

Since Annie's helper Rudolf broke a climber's code of honor by slyly racing past the person who had planned and paid for the expedition, most historians recognize Annie Smith Peck as the first woman to reach the top of a major mountain where no one had stood before.

HOW FAR NORTH CAN WE GO?
JOSEPHINE PEARY

"It's not too late to change your mind," Jo's father said.

Josephine Diebitsch Peary shook her head. While standing with her family on the deck of a ship in the New York City harbor, she held books and bouquets. She handed her father these going-away gifts and asked, "Will you take these to my cabin?"

Jo watched him leave with the last roses she'd smell for at least a year. He passed her husband, who was checking the supplies they'd packed for the Arctic. Robert looked as handsome as he had when they'd married five years before, when she was twenty-five. He was a tall man, with blue eyes almost the same shade as the Navy uniform he used to wear.

"Father worries too much," Jo said, turning back to her mother and her sister. "Last year in Greenland I learned how to sew fur clothes, which really kept us warm." She smoothed the skirt that covered her boots, remembering days when the temperature fell to fifty degrees below zero. Her hat was piled with feathers and bows, and her blouse puffed over her shoulders in a style that was fashionable that summer of 1893. "We're taking lumber and windowpanes to build a cabin. This time we've got barrels of oil to run a generator so we can put in electric lights. That will make the dark winter months more cheerful."

"Last time you weren't expecting a baby!" Mother said.

"One of the eleven men on the team is a doctor. We hired Mrs. Cross to cook, but she says she knows something about childbirth and such. Besides, Eskimos have babies, Mother." Jo didn't care to be like the Eskimos, or Inuit, as they called themselves. She wouldn't tuck her infant in the hood of her parka with a bit of moss to serve as a diaper. But she couldn't help admiring the way Inuit mothers didn't let their children keep them from traveling. Instead of staying near a cradle, the women went about their work with babies on their backs. They piled them onto sleds when it was time to leave one home to make another.

"God willing, you'll deliver your baby with no problems. But it's not easy to take care of an infant," Mother said, "while your husband's off looking for the North Pole."

"You won't even have a mailbox! We can't send you letters!" Marie said.

"I won't forget a word of your advice." Tenderly, Jo took her sister's hand. She would miss her parents, sister, brothers, and her old home in Washington, D.C. She loved the city's long green lawns, marble monuments, and most of all, the

Smithsonian Institution library, where she'd worked with her father.

"Mother, you didn't raise us to stay home." Jo touched her cheek. "You sailed from Germany to America when you were about my age."

"To be with your father," Mother said.

"As I will be with my husband." Jo let these words close the conversation.

Newspaper reporters warmed to her talk of wifely loyalty, but Jo kept quiet her other reasons for going north, just as she refrained from describing all the hardships. She'd found the four months without sun depressing. Some days she'd hiked for twelve hours, sometimes slogging waist-deep through cold water. She had been lonely when Robert and another man left for three months to dogsled to the northernmost part of Greenland, which they'd proven to be an island. Worst of all had been returning to the United States with only five men, instead of the six who'd left, and being able to give the missing man's family only a story about how they'd found his footprints near a deep crack in a glacier. But Jo was proud to have been the first white woman to cross the Arctic Circle. She loved the pale blue and white expanses of snow and sky. Cold winds had whistled and whispered, as if asking, *How strong are you?* A year in the far north hadn't been long enough to know. She was going back to find out.

Jo hugged her family and friends, then waved as the ship headed toward the Statue of Liberty. During the following days, Jo and Robert sailed along the New England coast, past Maine's great forests, to Canada, where the pines and spruces got shorter and more gnarled in the cold, salty air. Farther north, the ground was never soft enough for trees to take root, and the treeless shores told Jo they had crossed the Arctic Circle.

They headed east to Greenland, that huge island with its sad joke of a name for a place almost entirely covered with ice. No people lived in its interior, but Inuit lived by the sea, where they hunted seal and walrus, which they depended on for food and clothing. The ship stopped at several Inuit villages so Robert could buy sled dogs. Soon eighty-nine dogs were crowded below deck, and the ship became noisier and smellier.

Jo often stood on deck as they sailed past black cliffs and glaciers that shimmered pale blue, green, and pink. These towering glaciers looked still and silent but were slowly, slowly moving, carving away earth and melting into the sea. Sometimes the slow melting set off a sudden shift, and the ancient ice split. Chunks of ice collapsed into the sea, making icebergs that were often taller and wider than the white marble buildings in Washington, D.C. Others were even bigger. Their heavy bottoms sank below, and in the region's nearly constant fog even the most careful captain couldn't always avoid striking hidden ice.

Robert Peary wanted to get as far north as possible before the ocean froze over. Once the ice widened and thickened, it would be impossible to go on—or turn around. At Robert's urging, the captain found a way through the maze of ice floes. When ice covered the surface of the water, he ordered the ship to reverse, then shove forward to pound out a path. Storms began with little warning, and even bright, clear days were dangerous, for as sunlight reflected on distant ice, it was hard to tell nearby ice floes from the white glow of sky.

On the last day of July, the ship dropped anchor in a bay that was about halfway between the Arctic Circle and the North Pole. The yipping and howling dogs raced onto the pebble-covered shore. The explorers pitched tents, where everyone slept or hid from the mosquitoes that swarmed in the summer. Jo Peary and Mrs. Cross chopped ice from a glacier to melt into water for tea. They warmed up cans of baked beans.

During the next few weeks, the men built a lodge from wood they'd brought on the ship. Jo got out her rifle to hunt birds, which she cooked in stews. To make quilts, she collected baskets of down and feathers shed by eider ducks. Fluttery kicks often tapped the inside of her belly, and she felt both worry and hope for the first white baby who'd be born above the Arctic Circle.

The explorers were visited by Inuit men and women who'd taught the Pearys how to make and drive dogsleds, sew fur clothing, and survive in the north the last time they'd come to Greenland. Word had spread along the northwestern shore about the wood, pots and pans, guns, and ammunition that the Pearys had given the Inuit before sailing home last year, so other Inuit families came to settle nearby. They drove narwhal tusks into the ground to hold up their sealskin tents.

Once the lodge was built, Jo and Robert Peary moved in with the eleven men and Mrs. Cross. The shelter was rustic and crowded, but it was warmer than the tents and had a view of the blue bay, where white whales splashed and spouted. Behind the lodge, slow-melting glaciers released the salty scent of minerals that had been trapped in their ice for thousands of years.

The Inuit men helped Robert and his team build dogsleds. The women joined Jo in the lodge, making clothes for the expedition Robert hoped to lead in spring, when there would be sunlight but it would still be cold enough so that the icecap they'd walk on would be firm. The Inuit women softened seal leather by chewing on it, then stitched parkas and boots with sinews. They made socks from rabbit skin and trousers from polar-bear skin.

On September 12, 1893, Jo gave birth to a blue-eyed baby she named Marie Ahnighito Peary, in honor of her sister and of a woman who stitched a tiny snow suit from blue-fox fur, and small sealskin boots, which she shyly gave to Jo.

"She's so white!" Ahnighito exclaimed. She and other Inuit women touched the infant as if to make sure she wasn't made of snow. Even though they knew her skin, while paler, was just like theirs, they called her "Snow Baby." Jo didn't think of these short, brown-faced women as friends, yet she couldn't help liking anyone who marveled at her baby's ten perfect toes or enjoyed watching her wiggle her fingers.

As the women sewed, they taught Jo more of their language and talked about their lives. One day Jo asked them about a five-year-old boy she'd seen quietly watching the men build sleds. He looked dirtier than the other children, and lonely. The women told her that Koodluktoo's mother had died when he was an infant, then his father fell through the ice and died while hunting walrus. The women gave him spare scraps of food and cast-off clothing, but he had to wander from home to home with none to call his own.

"He's luckier than some orphans," Ahnighito said.

Jo knew Arctic life was harsh, and those too young or too old to care for themselves were sometimes left to die. She worried about the little boy but wasn't sure how to help. Then Matt Henson, one of the two men who'd been on the last Arctic expedition and the only black member of the team, said, "Why don't I scrub him down, cut his hair, and let him sleep under my bunk?"

"Of course." Jo smiled at Matt.

Jo enjoyed having Koodluktoo around, since he had a happy nature, which kept Jo from brooding, and he was always willing to watch the baby while she did chores. Marie Ahnighito was six weeks old when the first snows fell and ice began forming on the bay.

One mid-October morning, Jo heard a loud, thunderous crack. The floor shook. Mrs. Cross screamed, "The world is ending! Lord, have mercy!"

Jo snatched the baby from the cradle and ran outside. Waves, created by the impact of a huge block of ice that split from the glacier and toppled into the bay, flooded the shore. The rising water swept their two small boats and barrels of oil from the water's edge. Men leaped into the splintered ice and cold water, half running and half swimming to save the boats and barrels. The boats and most of the barrels were salvaged, but some had cracked, spilling oil that the explorers had hoped to use to warm and light the house. No electric lights would be put in, after all, and the lodge would be chilly.

Jo didn't complain. Robert had no patience for words that only seemed to sour the air. Besides, Jo had spent enough time in the far north not to despair over catastrophes that spared lives. The sun went down for the winter, and Jo stayed busy cooking, sewing, and caring for her baby. The thermometers read forty degrees below zero one day, thirty-five degrees below the next, though there were no numbers or words that could truly describe the cold. Jo kept a stove going and hung red blankets on the walls of the little bedroom she shared with her husband and baby, but she often preferred to be outdoors, where moving around helped her keep warm. Sometimes she left Marie with Mrs. Cross, called a dog, and took her rifle out to hunt for long-tailed duck or Arctic hare. More often, she strapped on snowshoes and headed across the snow to set or check her fox traps.

After four months of darkness, in the middle of February, a sunbeam streaked through a window. The baby raised her small hands, laughed, and tried to grab the golden stream. Not much later, Robert began loading the sleds with snowshoes, bedding, and rifles; with tins of biscuits, condensed milk, and pemmican, a mixture of dried beef, fruit, and fat. Jo looked toward land that was white, with muted blues, greens, and grays. She begged to go along.

"It will be even colder in the north," Robert said. "It's no place for a woman or a baby."

"You're taking Eskimo families!" Jo protested. She hadn't liked sleeping in an igloo, which she'd done last time they were here, but she was tired of the cabin walls. They had been built to keep out the cold, but moisture from people's bodies had collected and frozen on the walls, forming ice more than an inch thick.

"I can't get men to help me drive dogsleds unless they bring their wives," Robert said. "Their women have always helped with the dog teams and building igloos, and we'll need them to sew. With all the walking we'll be doing, our boots may need to be mended every night. You know a rip in a jacket needs to be fixed right away to keep us from frostbite, even death."

"I can sew!"

"Jo, I need a unified team. My men complain they have to mind their manners around you."

"Why, they belch and pull up their shirts to rub their bellies after a meal. And their language! If that's their best behavior, I'd hate to see them when I'm not around."

"I chose men for their courage, not their social graces," Robert said.

This wasn't their last argument, but in April Robert left with seven Americans and twelve Inuit men and women. Unless there was a blizzard, Jo bundled Marie in furs every day and took her out to enjoy the view of blue glaciers, black cliffs, and red-and-brown mountains. Marie played with some puppies. She laughed when Koodluktoo rolled round stones toward her. By the beginning of July, she had learned to say in Inuit *"nagga,"* or "no," and *"takoo,"* which meant "look!"

When small yellow poppies grew around green moss, a ship arrived to take them home. Jo told the captain and crew that they were still waiting for Robert and his team to return. Soon they did. Some men had blank, staring eyes. One had a frozen heel, and another's toes were frostbitten. Scraps of dead black skin peeled off Robert's cheeks. "There were lots of blizzards that kept us in igloos, and we ran low on food," he said. "We had to turn around before we reached the North Pole."

"Never mind." Jo began to hand him their baby but pulled Marie back when she squinted her eyes to cry. "Can you imagine, Marie has started talking!" Jo said. "Our brilliant baby knows more than a dozen words!"

"The hunting was poor, and the men complained of hunger," Robert said. "We need a smaller team. Next time I'm going with just Matt Henson, Hugh Lee, and some Eskimos."

"The ship is here to take us home."

"I'm not going, not when I haven't reached the Pole. Some of the icecap near the Pole is melting this time of year, but I'll stay in the lodge through the winter, then make another attempt when the sun returns next spring. Let the cowards go back on the ship! And you must take our baby home."

"We will stay here, too." Jo breathed the cold air, which hardened her determination.

"That's impossible. We don't have enough supplies, and when we set out for the North Pole, I couldn't leave you and the baby alone in the lodge."

"We could go north with you."

"Jo, think of the warm reunion we'll have when I return." Robert smiled, showing the gap between his front teeth, which she'd been fond of until now.

Before long, she boarded the ship to sail south. She waved at Koodluktoo, Ahnighito, and Robert, wondering if she'd ever see any of them again. Sails filled with wind still seemed to whisper, *How strong are you?* Whatever happened, Jo vowed to come back for the answer.

After the ship arrived in New York, Jo took a train to Washington, D.C., where she enjoyed showing off Marie to her family. The little girl now had curly brown hair like Jo's and a small gap between her front teeth like her father's. Sometimes Jo left Marie with her mother and traveled, giving lectures to earn money for her husband's quest. She arranged meetings with senators, military men, museum directors, and presidents of colleges and geographical societies—anyone who might help raise money and public interest in having an American flag fly at the North Pole. She offered generous donors a chance to have a glacier, or even a whole bay, named after them.

Despite several attempts over the next few years, Robert failed to reach the North Pole. He returned to the United States to raise funds and increase enthusiasm for his project. In 1897, Jo and Marie, who was almost four years old, sailed with him to northern Greenland. There they watched the sailors load onto the ship a big meteorite, which they'd take to New York City and sell to the American Museum of Natural History to help pay Robert's expenses. "I just want to try to get to the North Pole one more time," he said.

Jo didn't ask to go this time. She was expecting another child, and while taking along one baby on a dogsled seemed possible, looking after a lively young girl at the same time did not. She and Marie returned to the summer home the Pearys had bought on an island near Maine; then they stayed with Jo's family in Washington.

On January 7, 1899, Jo gave birth to a girl she named Francine. The baby was a happy distraction from her worry about Robert, whom she hadn't heard from in months. Jo took her two daughters to the beach, or wheeled the baby in a carriage while Marie raced across green lawns in air scented with roses and rhododendrons. But when Francine was six months old, she caught what a doctor said was cholera. Jo held her close and whispered, "Don't die. Your father's never even held you."

All her love and care couldn't save the baby's life. When people looked at Jo with pity and said, "Time heals all wounds," she wanted to punch them. Time! She had too much time already. She thought her grief could not get worse until that winter, when she learned that although Robert was alive, he had been caught in a snowstorm, slipped on ice, and badly hurt his chest. His feet had been ravaged by frostbite.

Jo told Marie, who was now six, "We're going back to Snowland as soon as it is warm enough for a ship to get through the ice." A ship was scheduled to sail north the next summer with supplies to last the explorers through another attempt to reach the North Pole. But Jo meant to bring her husband home.

"Your father's feet froze," she told Marie. "A doctor had to cut off seven toes to keep gangrene from spreading."

"Oh, my poor papa with only three toes!"

"We must help him." More than anything, Jo wanted her family of three to be together, though she'd have to wait a year until a ship could sail.

In July 1900, she and Marie boarded the *Windward*, a ship with a bow lined with iron so it could crash through ice. The first part of the journey was swift, but when they got near Greenland, they sailed slowly around blue-green icebergs. On sunny days, Marie jumped rope on the deck. The captain hung up a swing for her. During blizzards, the sailors climbed the rigging to chip off ice that sheathed the lines. Then Jo and Marie stayed in their cabin, which was so small they had to take turns standing by the single narrow bed. But it was a cozy place to work on Marie's spelling and arithmetic lessons, write in their diaries, play Parcheesi, or cuddle with the ship's cat. Marie sewed a pillow to stuff with Maine pine needles and give to her father.

One day while Jo was cutting paper dolls, Marie asked, "Is there really a pole where Papa is going?"

Jo shook her head. "It's only a point. It's just more snow and ice."

"Why does Papa want to go there?"

"Because no one else has been there."

"So when he gets there, he'll be famous?"

"That's what he wants. Glory." Jo knew her voice sounded flat.

"Isn't he lonely without us?" Marie asked.

"Of course he is. But Matt Henson has been on every North Pole attempt, and there are Eskimos and dogs. They all help one another."

"Will you cut me another paper doll?"

Jo picked up her scissors, grateful for the simple sound of paper being snipped.

As the days passed, thick fog made it hard for the sailors to steer, but when the fog lifted, ice closed over the sea. The ice grew wider and thicker, and the captain ordered the ship to smash through it. "Come on, *Windward*!" he shouted.

"You can do it!" Marie called.

Ice cracked and rumbled as the ship forged a path. The slush in its wake quickly froze. When the ship could no longer steam or sail ahead, the captain ordered sailors to climb overboard and hack open a path with axes and saws. Some sailors drilled holes in the ice, dropped in a bottle filled with gunpowder, and lit a long fuse. Chunks of ice exploded, but the ship moved forward only a few feet.

"It's time to find a safe harbor," the captain finally said.

The *Windward*'s sails were lowered near a village about twenty miles from the spot where Marie had been born. As ice thickened around the ship, it couldn't go forward and it couldn't turn back. It would be their home until the ice melted at the end of the eight-month winter.

Sailors stretched canvas over the deck to keep off falling snow. They piled snow around the ship so wind wouldn't whip through cracks and the cabins would stay warm. They carried food and tents to shore so they'd be prepared in case ice cracked the hull and the ship began to sink. Jo recognized some of the Inuit men who crossed the ice to see if they could help and who were hired as hunters. They knew nothing of her husband's fate.

Every day Jo and Marie scrambled over the ship's side to explore the ice. They made snowmen and forts and coasted on wooden skis from Norway, which the captain fastened together. They visited the village and met a few children. Marie showed them her fancy doll with eyes that blinked, while her new friends played with dolls carved from walrus tusks. The Inuit hunters had spread word about the ship, and Koodluktoo, who was now twelve, came to see them. Jo invited him to live aboard the ship as long as they were there.

When she heard of people in the village who were sick, Jo went to them with herbal remedies. At first she was simply

glad to have something useful to do, but she found that dol-
ing out medicine and advice, and seeing some people feel better, calmed her as nothing else had done since her baby died.
She spent more time in the village, where Marie played in the
snow with her friends.

One day Jo stopped a young woman who carried a baby
in her hood. Jo said hello and touched a strand of the baby's
hair, which poked out from a sealskin cap with fox fur
around the edge. The baby gazed at her, laughed, and waved
a fist.

"What a charming baby, so curious and strong! His father
must be proud," Jo said.

"His father is not here," the baby's mother said.

"Has he gone hunting? Without you?" Jo asked.

"His father is a white man, big and brave."

"An explorer?" Jo's face warmed. She realized she'd been
naïve not to guess the unmarried men on her husband's team
might ease their loneliness with Inuit women.

"The leader. I drove dogsleds with him way, way north.
They call him Pearyaksoah."

The baby smiled again, and Jo noticed a small gap between his front teeth. A cold wind slapped her face. She heard
the crack of splitting ice.

"Maybe you know him?" the woman said.

"No," Jo said. "I don't know him." She pulled the edges
of her coat tighter and strode toward Marie. She said, "It's
time to go home."

"Mama, I'm playing!" Marie protested.

Jo grabbed her hand and led her back to the frozen-in
ship.

Snow fell thick and often during the next few dark weeks. Shifting ice made the ship tilt so that the floors slanted.

As the sun returned in March, Jo visited the village. Someone told her that the young woman with the baby had become very ill.

"Please bring your medicines to Aleqasina," the woman said. "We think she is dying."

Jo crawled inside the narrow opening of a stone-and-turf house. The young woman breathed heavily. Her forehead gleamed with sweat. Jo thought of how this young woman had traveled with her husband, when she'd been left behind. A healthy baby lay curled beside her, while her baby, Francine, was dead.

"There is nothing I can do," Jo said. "I am not a nurse."

She returned to the ship and looked at the ice. When she heard voices, she turned to watch Koodluktoo showing Marie how to play cat's cradle by twisting sinew strings between their hands. They laughed as they made the shapes of a raven, rabbit, and fox. Jo spoke a few words to the orphan and to her daughter, then turned back toward the ice. She wondered what would happen to Aleqasina's baby if his mother died. He might wander from home to home, wearing torn clothes and asking for food no one else wanted. He might even be killed.

Jo went back to the sick woman's home. Calling upon every bit of her strength, she opened a bottle of medicine, lifted a spoon, poured the liquid, and held it toward the woman's lips.

During the following weeks Jo returned often to care for Aleqasina. Her heart, which had felt broken, began to heal.

She had fun when Koodluktoo took her and Marie for a ride on a dogsled. After the ice melted in a nearby bay, Koodluktoo taught Marie how to paddle a kayak. Jo felt proud of her brave daughter.

In May, mist rose as ice around the ship cracked and shifted. One day Jo was standing on the deck when she heard uneven footsteps. She turned to see Robert struggling to slide one leg after the other. His eyes looked dull. Black lines on his gums outlined his teeth, an early sign of scurvy. Jo remembered the dreamer she'd married, and opened her arms.

"Where's the baby?" Robert asked as they hugged.

"You didn't get my letters? Francine died." Jo shook her head as if she could whisk away the memory and called, "Marie!"

The girl had already spotted her father. She looked from him to her mother.

Robert crouched down and spread his arms. "Come here, Marie Ahnighito!"

Marie stayed where she was.

"Have I changed that much?" Robert asked.

"All of us have changed." Jo held her back straight in the brisk wind. "You've been gone almost three years."

"I'm seven," Marie said. She ran to her swing.

Jo looked from their vanishing daughter down to Robert's boots. "Let me see your feet."

He shook his head.

"I'm not a coward," Jo said. "I can face things."

Robert looked at her, sat down on the deck, and tugged at his boots. He peeled off his socks to reveal eight blackened stumps where his toes had been.

Jo touched her mouth. She had loved those eight toes, now gone.

"Is it that bad?" he asked.

"No." Jo shook her head. "It's just that we heard you'd lost seven toes, not eight." She swallowed hard and lightly touched one ankle. Her voice sounded hoarse as she said, "You must come home with us."

"Not yet."

She pulled away her hand. "It's time to stop, Robert. You've been farther north than anyone else in the world. Why can't that be enough?"

"That wasn't my goal. I don't want my name to go down in history as a failure."

"Books are full of stories about explorers who never found what they were looking for but who made it possible for others." Jo noticed that Robert's skin had a pale green cast. He had punched extra notches in his belt to hold up his trousers.

"The ship has enough supplies for us to stay and try again next spring. I'm bound to get there next time," he said.

"Unless you die trying."

"Better that than turn around."

"No! It's not better!" Silence followed Jo's words. She looked for Marie and saw the empty swing blowing in the cold breeze.

"I just want to try once more! If I don't go next spring, someone else may reach the North Pole before I do."

"What difference would that make?"

"All the difference."

Why couldn't he tell when a dream had become an obsession?

"I'm going to look for Marie," Jo said. Wind stung her cheeks, and she realized that she had the answer to the question it seemed to ask. Whether or not her husband came along, she was going home as soon as the ice around the ship melted. She knew how strong she was.

—

Her husband remained in the Arctic while Josephine Diebitsch Peary (1863–1955) returned to Washington with their daughter. Jo sailed up to meet him the following summer, and between attempts to reach the North Pole, Robert sometimes visited his family. Jo gave birth to Robert Peary, Jr., in 1903, and then she and her children began spending less time in Washington and more time at their summer home on a Maine island.

In 1909, Jo got word that Robert Peary, Matthew Henson, and four Inuit men named Ootah, Seeglo, Ooqueah, and Egingwah had achieved Robert's dream of twenty-three years. That same year, Dr. Frederick Cook also claimed to have reached the North Pole. Whether either man had truly arrived at the farthest northern point has been debated ever since. Some researchers have noted that Robert Peary's sightings were vague. His statements about times and places appear inaccurate, and his description of arriving at the North Pole was not included in his diary but written on a piece of paper that might have been inserted later.

Throughout Josephine Peary's long life, she never publicly doubted her husband's word. Their daughter Marie Peary Stafford (1893–1978) also served as advocate for her father while living a full life that included marriage, two children, travel, and a career as a writer. In recognition of Josephine Peary's five trips to the Arctic, and perhaps for the long silence she kept about some of the costs of exploration, the National Geographic Society awarded her its highest honor, its Medal of Achievement, in 1955.

HOW CAN A CONTINENT BE CROSSED?
ARNARULUNGUAQ

The Arctic air was cold, but the igloo was warmed by a fire. Arnarulunguaq began her story with the word *Itaq*.

The man who'd come from far away, but who spoke the language of the Inuit, translated her word in his notebook as "Long, long ago." Knud Rasmussen had a family across the sea, but he'd spent years learning to survive in the far north. He could drive a dogsled, hunt seal and walrus, and listen to a story without interrupting.

"Nerrivik was an orphan." Arnarulunguaq looked down at the boot she was mending, then continued. "People wanted to find better hunting grounds. They lashed together kayaks to make a raft and paddled out to sea, leaving behind poor Nerrivik. She swam to the raft and clung to the edge. Men chopped off her fingers. Nerrivik sank in the cold, salty water. Her broken fingers became the first seals and walrus. She turned into the goddess of the sea. When she is happy, she tells seals and walrus to swim to the sea's surface and we have food. When she is angry, she helps animals hide."

Arnarulunguaq put down her needle to show that this was the end of the story. Knud read what he'd written in his notebook. Arnarulunguaq nodded, indicating that he'd caught her words. But he'd missed the sadness in her voice, the places where she'd paused and memory had mixed with myth. Arnarulunguaq was twenty-eight. She had been married for ten years, in which she had been happy despite her disappointment that she'd never borne a child. But she never forgot her childhood, when, as an orphan, she'd had to scavenge for seaweed, mussels, and scraps of tough meat thrown to the sled dogs. Her fur parka and trousers were always torn. She'd wandered from one stone or snow house to another, where people let her sleep in entryways but never by the warm lamps in the centers of their homes.

Knud Rasmussen thanked her for the story. He wrote down many others in the northern Greenland village, where he stayed until the days grew light and ravens returned.

In the spring of 1921, he and the villagers gathered pots, knives, harpoons, skins used for bedding and tents, and the precious worn poles made from driftwood that would hold up tents. Everyone sledded to another village, where Knud found mail left by a whaling ship. His eyes looked big and round as he waved a letter from the King of Denmark. Arnarulunguaq and the people from her village settled on a rock to listen.

"The King of my country has asked me to cross the sea to collect ancient Inuit stories," Knud said. "I'll talk to people on the many islands along Canada's northeastern coast. Then I'll cross the northern coast of Canada, walking and dogsledding more than two thousand miles to Alaska. We believe life will change as more ships come to the far north. Even airplanes may fly here, bringing new ideas. We want to keep your stories from being forgotten."

"Everything changes." Arnarulunguaq looked at the ice, which turned to water, then turned back to ice.

"But not everything has to disappear," Knud said. "When men stop spending hours waiting for a seal, they will not teach patience to their sons. When women get ready-made clothes, words that once passed between mothers and daughters while sewing will be lost." He unrolled a map and pointed to a curved line called the Arctic Circle, which ran through Greenland and Canada. "We want to know the cold, treeless lands better than anyone. We want to be the first to cross them on foot from the Atlantic Ocean to the Pacific! I'll need people to help hunt, cook, care for the dogs, and sew. The King will send flour, tea, and cans of condensed milk here so those you leave behind won't go hungry."

"I will help!" Arnarulunguaq grabbed her husband's hand.

Iggianguaq shook his head and took away his hand. "How can we leave?" He looked past the pale blue lichen to the black cliffs. "Each rock has a name here. Every hill has a story."

"We will come back!" Arnarulunguaq said.

"Will we meet this king?" asked Miteq, a young unmarried man who was Arnarulunguaq's cousin. "Who is so good to send children cans of milk and so curious about our stories?"

"He will want to thank those who help," Knud said.

"I will go," Miteq said.

Arnarulunguaq looked hopefully at her husband.

"Why should we leave behind everything we know?" Iggianguaq said. "Why should we change?"

"Snow houses are never built to last forever. Tents are meant to be rolled up," Arnarulunguaq said. "Even stone-and-earth houses are meant to be lived in for a while, then left for someone else."

Iggianguaq didn't answer, but a few days later he agreed to go along with her, Knud, Miteq, and two couples who left their children in the care of grandparents, aunts, and uncles. They sledded south to the biggest village Arnarulunguaq had

ever seen. Wooden boats and umiaks—small boats made of walrus skins—rested onshore. Two tall ships were anchored in the bay. Knud told them these ships had stopped to trade canned goods and ammunition for sealskins. One would take them to Canada. About a dozen wooden houses, one decked with Denmark's red-and-white flag, stood near stone houses covered with gray-and-green moss. Arnarulunguaq heard people coughing.

Knud stayed in a house with five scientists from Denmark, who were joining the expedition to study rocks, plants, and animals. Arnarulunguaq, Iggianguaq, Miteq, and the two Inuit couples put up their sealskin tents near the edge of town.

While waiting for the ship to be ready to carry them to Canada, the Inuit came down with influenza. For days they were too weak and dizzy to leave the tent. Then Arnarulun-

guaq felt well enough to find Knud and make sure he didn't leave without them. When she returned to the tent, she felt a strange silence amid the sounds of coughing. Her husband had died.

Arnarulunguaq ran out of the tent and raced to the shore. She cursed Nerrivik, who had power over who would live and who would die. She dared the goddess of the sea to show her face. Arnarulunguaq stood on the shore for hours, but no fingerless hands rose from the sea. Even the seals sunning themselves on rocks did not look her way. She grieved for the man who'd driven the dogs she'd hitched to sleds, hunted for the seals she'd cooked, and found the stones she'd piled into houses. She stood on the shore until her sorrow lightened, and she remembered that she had strong legs, arms, and a beating heart.

Knud came to find her. "I am sorry about Iggianguaq," he said.

Arnarulunguaq felt embarrassed for Knud, who didn't know it was wrong to speak the name of the dead. It could hold his spirit to the earth. She nodded, and for a while they let the silence be. Then Arnarulunguaq asked, "Do you have a family?"

"I have a wife and three children back in Denmark."

"Is it your people's way to leave your family?" she asked.

"Sometimes." Knud spoke quietly. "Yes." Music returned to his voice as he said, "I've wanted to take this trip since I left college, for almost twenty years! But I can't do it alone. Now I suppose you will go back."

"No." The place she'd left behind already seemed smaller. Arnarulunguaq looked across the sea, which was not only the home of seals, walrus, and Nerrivik. It was a way to another world. "No, I will not go back."

Arnarulunguaq and the other Inuit were still sick when they boarded a ship early in September 1921. Storms raged, and the sled dogs, crowded together below deck, howled. The captain couldn't keep the ship on course in the fog, but he kept heading west through white-capped waves. They reached an island in northeastern Canada, where the explorers set up tents. The men hunted hare. Arnarulunguaq collected water from a lake, tended the fire in a stone lamp, and prepared meals. She cared for the dogs and sewed fur socks and boots when the old ones got worn.

As the days grew darker, ice turned rivers and bays into roads. The Danish scientists split into two groups, each with an Inuit couple to help hunt and cook, and left on dogsleds to collect plants, stones, shells, and animal bones. Arnarulunguaq, Knud, and Miteq set out to find people who would tell them old stories. They dogsledded from one river or bay to another and stayed in a village long enough for the shapes of hills to become familiar.

Arnarulunguaq spotted orphans by their lonely eyes and torn parkas. She taught them games and mended their leggings. She helped them cut fishing holes in ice that had darkened from blue to black as it grew thicker. Together, they watched Inuit men who waited beside the breathing holes seals made in the ice. Sometimes the men stood for hours, harpoon in hand, hardly moving, for even a slight sound or motion could make the seal turn and swim away.

Arnarulunguaq met children who'd been adopted, often from parents who couldn't care for a baby, and she missed her husband all over again. She wished they'd had the luck to meet someone who had offered them a child.

In the evenings, she told people about the curious King who had gold and a palace but wanted their stories, too. Knud opened his notebook and waited as quietly as the hunters waited for seals. People liked the tall man with wide eyes, but perhaps they wouldn't have told Knud their tales, jokes, and songs so easily if Arnarulunguaq hadn't widened her eyes or tilted her chin to make a smooth path for his words. She laughed at jokes. She touched the hands of someone who'd told a sad story. Some stories were familiar, and some were new. Many people spoke of an orphaned girl with broken fingers, though details varied and the goddess of the sea had different names.

The brief summer arrived. As Arnarulunguaq, Miteq, and Knud walked, their boots brushed rosebay, Arctic heather, and red berries. Eider ducks, Canadian geese, Arctic loons, and gulls flew over tundra that turned yellow with dandelions and mountain avens. Before long, more snow fell, and the explorers traveled to other villages, where Knud traded needles, knives, axes, nails, and matches for new dogs to pull their sleds.

By the time sunlight returned for their second spring in Canada, they had run out of flour, tea, sugar, and canned food. The scientists were back and ready to take samples of rocks, plants, shells, fossils, and carved antlers or bones, which Knud called artifacts, to Denmark's King. The two Inuit couples missed their children. They wanted to go back to Greenland.

"Do you want to go home, too?" Knud asked Arnarulunguaq and Miteq. He explained that they would be gone more than a year if they chose to explore the top of Canada, where it would be hard to tell the edge of the continent. Arnarulunguaq knew that ice disguised the boundaries between sea and shore. Journeys were shaped by weather, hunting, and people met along the way. "We promised to help," she said.

"You can't go on alone," Miteq pointed out.

The three of them set forth, sometimes joined by Inuit men Knud hired to help them hunt. They met members of the Royal Canadian Mounted Police, Hudson's Bay Company traders, and missionaries. Knud stopped at a village where the Inuit had traded fox furs for gramophones, which played operas and tangos. The Inuit wore cotton shirts and bright woolen shawls over their traditional skin parkas and pants. Shiny parts of broken watches, along with fox teeth and crow claws worn for protection, dangled from leather strips around their necks. Knud asked them for stories, and worried about the changes outsiders were bringing to this land.

"The rifles from traders help people hunt," Arnarulunguaq said. "Everyone needs to eat."

"The guns let them kill more reindeer and caribou at first, but the noise scares away even more animals," Knud said. "Your people did fine with arrows and harpoons for thousands of years. The traders always want more fox skins and bear furs. They're not like your people, who take only what they can eat and use for clothing. The traders won't ever have enough."

"Everyone wants more of something. You want more stories," Arnarulunguaq said. She looked at his piles of notebooks. She was curious about the words on paper, which seemed to hide or hold secrets, like ice on the surface of a river. She said, "I want to learn to read and write."

He shook his head. "Your people have always told stories. You don't need to write them down."

"Spoken words disappear."

"Maybe someday I will teach you," he said. "We have so much to do already."

Knud asked Miteq and another man to drive a dogsled south toward Hudson Bay to get supplies while he and Arnarulunguaq traveled another way. They planned to meet in fall at Queen Maud Gulf, where they'd still have more than half of Canada left to cross.

Most mornings, Arnarulunguaq hitched dogs to a sled. She balanced on the runners, gripping the uprights and an ivory ring tied with leads attached to five dogs. "Go!" she cried.

The world seemed to burst open as the dogs bolted forward. The strongest dog ran in front, while the others spread in a fan shape. Particles of flying snow stung Arnarulunguaq's face. On hills or long, smooth stretches of snow, she leaped off the runners and ran between them to lighten the weight pulled by the dogs.

Sometimes they reached villages where people shared houses and told stories, which Knud wrote down. Sometimes they found only snow and had to build a house before they could rest. They cut hardened snow into blocks, which they piled in a circle. They set more blocks of snow on these, slanting each slightly toward the middle to spiral up to a domed roof. Inside the igloo, Arnarulunguaq and Knud gently plucked icicles from each other's eyelashes. They rubbed each other's feet to warm them. They began to share a bed of reindeer skins like husband and wife.

"This must end when our journey is over," Knud said. "When I married, my wife understood that I'd be gone, sometimes for years, but that I'd return."

Arnarulunguaq nodded. She knew a person must go back to where she or he came from.

Summer began. Breezes near their faces were cool, but it was warmer close to earth, so that Arctic willow grew almost to their ankles. Petals of yellow poppies were smaller than fingernails.

They reached an island and found remnants of twelve stone houses that Knud guessed had been abandoned a thousand years before. Swans nested by the river. Knud decided to stay there for a while. He found stones, and Arnarulunguaq stacked them to build a stone-and-earth house of their own. He sketched and studied the ancient sites. Arnarulunguaq spread nets to catch trout and salmon. She picked red berries, blueberries, and crowberries, which made her mouth pucker with their tangy sweetness.

In fall, they heard a whisper and crackle, softer than breath, as ice formed on the lake's still surface. Snow fell. They filled the entryway of their house with rocks and rubble to keep out evil spirits, hitched up the dogs, and continued west. They met Miteq a few months after they'd planned. By then, Arnarulunguaq had come to feel life growing inside her.

The dark months began again. The moon circled the sky, never seeming to set. They still had about a thousand miles to walk and sled to the border of Alaska. Arnarulunguaq, Miteq, and Knud crossed long fields of ice that had melted and frozen over and over again, expanding, contracting, and leaving blocks of ice with jagged edges jammed together, rising every which way. They had to find a path among these, or climb without tripping or falling. They reached parts of the earth that were new to them, but they asked the old questions: *What will we eat? Where can we sleep?* Arnarulunguaq wondered: *Will my baby be born safely?* Each day they found a way to stay alive.

When their hands and feet turned numb, they cut blocks of snow to build a round house. They fed the gray-and-white dogs, then left them to sleep curled in the same shape as their igloo.

Blizzards sometimes kept the three of them inside for days at a time. Then Arnarulunguaq moved her needle in small circles, mending boots that were worn by ice and blood. Knud told stories about maple trees with leaves that turned red and yellow in fall, and spruces and pines that stayed green all year long. He said, "Some trees even give food—butternuts and apples!" Arnarulunguaq tried to imagine how these might taste.

After the sky cleared, they traveled again. Knud had maps, but vast stretches had no names. During the dark months, they looked to stars for guidance. When it was light, the bottoms of clouds, which reflected dark rivers and rock, made a picture of where they'd come from. Sometimes Knud, Arnarulunguaq, and Miteq found cairns, or piles of stones, where explorers had stashed old diaries, maps, and food. Some Inuit had stacked stones in the shape of a person with arms akimbo to serve as guides and warnings, pointing out safe places to cross rivers, good hunting grounds, and the depths of snow. Even when Arnarulunguaq couldn't read the messages, it was good to know that someone had once been this way.

Sometime at the end of 1923 or early in 1924, the explorers stopped in a village, where Arnarulunguaq gave birth. Two women held her; one woman cut the cord. Arnarulunguaq destroyed her old clothes, following the way of women before her. She put on new fur trousers and a parka, slipped the baby into her hood, and continued on her way.

"He cries because he wants a name," she told Knud.

"You will find a name later," he said.

She thought it was strange to wait, but that might be his people's way. When she praised the baby's bright eyes and plump knees, Knud didn't pay much attention. Arnarulunguaq was too happy to mind. The back of her neck was always warm now. Small eyelashes fluttered against her skin. It became more tiring to walk, but the world seemed full of marvels, which she pointed out to the baby on her back.

When their path was blocked by a river, they found an ice floe, which they rode to the other shore. Once, when they were caught in a blizzard, Miteq spotted a cave in a cliff. They leaned their sleds against the rock and climbed them like ladders into the cave.

Eventually they passed fence posts that marked the boundary between Canada and Alaska. Soon they crossed more tundra than ice, and met more trappers, traders, missionaries, and gold miners than Inuit.

On the northern coast of Alaska, they traded their dogs and sleds for an umiak. As they paddled through rough seas, Arnarulunguaq kept checking her hood to make sure her baby didn't bounce into the cold waves and Nerrivik's finger-less hands. At night, they set up their tent, where she took the baby out of her hood. He struggled to sit up, then laughed when he tipped over. Arnarulunguaq scooted just out of arm's reach, then called, "Come!"

The baby babbled as he learned to crawl.

After more than three years, the journey was almost over. The three explorers got a ride on a fishing boat. They stood on the deck, gazing at green hills and snowcapped mountains.

"Look!" Arnarulunguaq told her baby, pointing to whales.

"The King will be happy about all we've collected," Miteq said.

"He will be thankful for your help," Knud said. "And amazed. We've crossed Arctic Canada, which stretches more than two thousand miles, but with all the circling we did, we traveled much farther. Maybe twenty thousand miles. That's almost the width of the world at the equator."

"Is that where we will go next?" Arnarulunguaq asked. "Where you said the water is always warm?"

"We will sail south to Seattle, in the state of Washington, then take a train across the United States to New York City," Knud said. "Then we'll sail to Europe."

"Oh, what our baby will see!" Arnarulunguaq exclaimed.

Knud's face darkened. "You can't bring the baby to Denmark. People in my old home would not understand. We agreed that we would be together only for this journey."

Arnarulunguaq had said that before they'd had a child. Now the world had changed.

"What can I do?" she asked. "I can't leave my baby behind. I can't live where I know no one."

Knud moved away from the railing that circled the deck. A wave smacked the boat, loud as a knife falling on a girl's clinging hands. Arnarulunguaq understood she'd have to answer her own question. She reached back to touch her baby's hand and promised, "I will take care of you."

They reached Nome, Alaska, late in the summer of 1924. At the edge of town, Inuit lived in tents or umiaks that they'd turned upside down to make dome-topped shelters. The explorers set up their tent, then walked to the center of Nome, where streets were paved with wooden planks. Rectangular houses, taverns, churches, schools, and shops were crammed close together. Knud read signs and explained that money was used here more than trading. "You've never seen a restaurant, have you? It's a place where someone with coins or bills can get a meal."

"Can we go in?" Miteq asked.

"Why not?" Knud said.

They walked into a restaurant, where a man behind the counter glared at Arnarulunguaq and Miteq. "We don't serve Eskimos," he said.

"Come on!" Knud's face turned red with anger as he linked his arms through theirs and rushed outside. "So this is civilization. Who do they think lived here first? Never mind, we'll find another place to eat."

"I'm not hungry." Arnarulunguaq broke away. She headed back toward the tents and overturned boats at the edge of town. She heard coughing as she passed people huddled on a street, then more coughing from behind the doors of wooden houses. She wondered: *How could I care for my baby if I fell ill? What would happen to him if I died?*

The baby patted her face.

"Don't worry," Arnarulunguaq said. "My beautiful baby." Then she imagined her baby growing into a small, hungry child in ragged clothes, holding out his hand to beg for scraps. People might let him sleep in entryways but never by the warm lamps in the centers of their homes. Arnarulunguaq remembered what that was like.

A young Inuit woman stopped and asked, "Are you all right?"

"Yes," Arnarulunguaq just barely managed to say.

"What a sweet baby!" The woman gently touched his nose, then looked at Arnarulunguaq and asked, "Are you alone? Are you lost?"

"No."

"Where did you come from?"

"Another village." Arnarulunguaq didn't want to say she'd crossed a continent and sound as if she were bragging when this woman was being so kind.

"Then you must need a place to stay. My husband and I have room."

"I'm not alone."

"Good! We have room for everyone. Please come!"

Arnarulunguaq suddenly hated the tent she shared with Knud and Miteq. She found them there, and a few days later all three moved into the two-room house furnished with wooden tables, chairs, and a stove. The woman and her husband told her about how, in a place without seals or caribou, they found food. They played with the baby and talked of their sorrow at not having a baby of their own. Knud read newspapers and said that the Inuit of Alaska had been granted the right to vote in U.S. elections that year.

While waiting for a ship due to come in a few weeks, Knud spent days talking to the Inuit who lived along Nome's border. He traded the last of his needles and nails for the feathers, bones, and teeth the Inuit wore for protection, and assured them that though he took the charms, the magic would stay with them.

Arnarulunguaq usually remained in the house, where her baby liked to crawl under chairs and tables. The couple sang old songs to him, and one day they brought home a red ball. They rolled it across the wooden floor and watched it bounce from one wall to another. The baby stared. They rolled the ball toward the baby, who laughed with his mouth wide open. He fell forward to catch the ball, then laughed some more, as if he'd caught the moon.

"If you had a child, would you teach him how to read and write?" Arnarulunguaq asked.

"We would send him to school," the woman said.

"Would you teach him how to hunt and row a boat, too?" Arnarulunguaq asked. "Would you show your child what color ice is safe to walk on?"

"Yes," they said. "Yes. Here a child can learn the new ways and the old ways as well."

Arnarulunguaq didn't have to ask if they would love the baby. She knew they already did. Her child might learn how snow made roads for sleds and how to pile blocks of snow into round houses. He might speak English and the language of the Inuit, too. He could learn old stories and imagine new ones.

When the time came to board the ship, Arnarulunguaq didn't look back. But she missed the warm circle of breath on her neck.

Arnarulunguaq, Miteq, and Knud sailed to Seattle. They took a train across the United States. They sped past mountains, deserts, farmlands, and forests of evergreens with pointed tops. Other trees had brown leaves, and some had no leaves at all. Their bare branches seemed to scrape the sky, which looked smaller here. Arnarulunguaq missed the soft colors and smooth lines of the land where she'd been born.

"The leaves will come back," Knud said.

He talked about spring, but Arnarulunguaq turned away. Now she didn't want anything from this man who had walked thousands of miles and written thousands of pages so the world wouldn't lose old stories, but who was willing to lose almost everything else. The train was too noisy, warm, and smoky. Arnarulunguaq didn't even like the way the skies turned dark every night and lightened every morning. She closed her eyes and remembered how her baby had opened his hands and toppled onto the red ball. She wondered if that still made him laugh. Had he tried to balance with his hand on a chair yet, maybe even taken a first step? Did he ever dream of her? Arnarulunguaq knew that her questions would not be answered.

In New York City, she petted horses that pulled wagons with apples or bottles of milk. She rode trolley cars, watched a movie, and climbed a skyscraper. The three explorers sailed to Denmark, where the King looked through Knud's note-

books and boxes of carved bones, feathers, and stones. He
gave Arnarulunguaq and Miteq each a branch of a beech, his
favorite tree, and a gold medal. The King was kind, but he
wasn't as curious as they had expected. He didn't ask them
one question about their journey.

"I've arranged for a fishing ship to take you home," Knud
told them a few days later. He whispered to Arnarulunguaq,
"You did the right thing. Sharing children is the old way."

"It is the old way. But it was the wrong thing to do."
Arnarulunguaq plucked a leaf from the branch the King had
given her. The leaf had been green and soft, but now it was
brittle. It crumbled in her hand.

Soon she and Miteq boarded a ship that headed toward
the land where she'd known the names of every person, rock,
and hill. As they sailed through cold, dark water, Arnarulunguaq stood on the deck and watched icebergs shimmer. One
day she thought she heard her name rise from the waves and
wind. Two seals swam to the ocean's surface. Their brown
eyes shone and blinked.

Arnarulunguaq stepped back as Nerrivik's head and fingerless hands seemed to rise from the sea. "You can't take
me!" She stamped her foot. Why should she be afraid when
she'd survived so much already? She had crossed a continent.
She had seen wonders, and she had known the greatest grief.
Like the goddess of the sea, Arnarulunguaq knew she could
go anywhere.

—

*Since Arnarulunguaq (1895?–?), whose name is sometimes
spelled Anarulunguaq, couldn't write, what little we know*

about her ends when she and Knud Rasmussen parted in 1924, at the end of what is called the Fifth Thule Expedition. While his valuable journals and books reveal much about the vanishing ways of the Inuit in Greenland, Canada, and Alaska, among the thousands of published pages there is only a little about Arnarulunguaq and almost nothing about the child he fathered. We don't know if Arnarulunguaq married again, had more children, or did any further traveling; we don't even know when she died. We can only guess that she never forgot her losses but was proud of her remarkable journey.

HOW DEEP IS THE EARTH?
ELISABETH CASTERET

Elisabeth Casteret enjoyed a view of clouds beneath her feet. Still, climbing snowcapped mountains wasn't her only goal. She wanted to explore the deep, hidden parts of the earth. In the summer of 1926, Elisabeth climbed the Pyrenees Mountains with her husband, Norbert Casteret, and his mother and brother. No one had yet discovered a cave in the mountains that divided Spain from France. The Casterets had searched before and found no way inside the mountains, but Elisabeth felt certain that dark pathways wound under the high rocks.

"Could that be a cave?" She pointed while shielding her eyes from the glare of sunlight on snow.

"Let's go see," Norbert said. They slammed down their hobnailed boots so they wouldn't slip on the ice. They found some exposed rocks, but no way past them. They cut toe-holds in the ice with axes as they headed toward another dark spot that turned out to be only a shadow on the snow. They kept on trudging through snowdrifts. Elisabeth knew disappointment was a path to discovery.

"Look!" She headed toward a blue-black space between two clouds, where they found a rock ledge with an opening beneath it. Elisabeth, Norbert, and his mother and brother shouted with joy. They spent several hours digging out snow to make a way into the cave.

Elisabeth checked the pockets of her knee-length skirt for her rosary beads and spare candles. Everyone lit lanterns and slogged knee-deep through the icy slush inside the cave. When snowdrifts blocked their way, they shoveled through them. Finally the dark tunnel widened to a hall that arced over a frozen underground lake. The ice was so clear that Elisabeth could see pebbles frozen twelve feet below the surface.

The dazzling hall reminded her of meeting Norbert two years earlier, when she was nineteen. He'd brought her to a cave where the darkness was deeper than anywhere on the earth's surface. They lit candles, and light flickered on crystal towers that seemed to be their very own castle. By the time they were married in a small church in Saint-Gaudens, the town where they lived in southern France, they had already shown their mutual trust by shinnying down ropes, each held by the other, into caverns.

Now Elisabeth grabbed Norbert's hand and ran to the ice. Waving lanterns with their unclasped hands, they skidded over the skating rink under the earth. Their laughter echoed against the smooth rock walls.

Soon they left the cave to camp under the stars. Norbert's mother and brother went home the next morning, but Elisabeth and Norbert ate a breakfast of bread and chocolate, slung knapsacks over their shoulders, looped ropes over their arms, and returned to the ice cave. Since they'd already shoveled out snow, they had more time to explore. They strapped on the steel helmets that Norbert had worn in the Great War and scurried through narrow tunnels, where the air temperature was well below the freezing point. They bumped into icicles, which fell and shattered. They passed glaciers formed by snow that had melted, frozen again, and compacted over thousands of years. The earth was always changing, and some signs of these changes could be seen only from below its surface.

At the end of the tunnel loomed a tall frozen waterfall.

"Do you think we can climb this icy Niagara?" Norbert asked.

"Why not?" Elisabeth said.

They roped themselves together and pounded their ice picks into the frozen cascade as they climbed. They reached the top, then entered more tunnels formed by water freezing and melting over and over again. Elisabeth and Norbert discovered a frozen waterfall the height of a seven-story building and climbed it.

They stopped for a lunch of long crusty bread, cheese, and clear glacial water. While they were walking, they had to be alert to falling rocks and hard-to-see holes, but they relaxed as they sat under overhanging rocks, which probably had been there for thousands of years and were unlikely to fall any time soon. After slicing the bread and cheese, Elisabeth and Norbert extinguished their lanterns to save fuel.

The darkness was perfect. It was like nothing on earth, where even at night moon- or starlight could seep through cracks in shuttered windows.

After lunch, they relit their lanterns and found a way to a rock ledge. Elisabeth bent over so that Norbert could climb onto her shoulders. He stepped quickly, pulled himself up to the narrow rock outcropping, and leaned down to give her a hand up. They climbed an ice-glazed wall that led to a passageway, which they crawled through. A film of water coated the ice and soaked Elisabeth's skirt, the knees of her wool stockings, and the elbows of her jacket.

Light from their lanterns fell on stalactites that had formed as water dripped from the ceiling for thousands of years. Some water had spattered, slowly dissolving limestone, which concentrated, crystallized, and grew into a calcite tower. Called stalagmites, some of these towers almost reached the ceiling. Other crystal forms spread in the shapes of fans, coral, and shrubs.

"It's like being inside a diamond," Elisabeth said.

There were still parts of the cave they hadn't entered, but Norbert picked up a rock and scratched his name in the wall so that if other cavers followed, they'd know someone had gotten there first. Elisabeth also scratched words on the rock.

"Did you write your name, too?" Norbert asked.

"I wrote something more lasting." She tucked the lantern behind her back, so her words disappeared in the darkness. She smiled to herself. "You'll see when we come back."

They planned to return to the first ice cave ever found in the Pyrenees Mountains, but during the following years they chose instead to explore caves close enough to their home to

reach by bicycle. Norbert earned money by writing books about the ways in which caves show that the earth has been shaped by water, weather, and time. Geologists depended on the Casterets' work, and ever since a few cave paintings had been found at the end of the nineteenth century, historians had become more interested in life underground.

Elisabeth gave birth to Gilberte, then to her second daughter, Maud. The Casterets knew it was unsafe to explore a cave alone, so whenever Elisabeth was so far along in a pregnancy that her belly kept her from squeezing through tunnels, Norbert's mother often joined her son in caves. When the children were old enough to be left with their grandmother, Elisabeth and Norbert searched for intriguing holes in nearby beech and pine woods.

One morning in 1932, Elisabeth, Norbert, his mother, and the two little girls set out from the village of Labastide. Elisabeth raced Gilberte up a hill. Norbert carried Maud, who waved at sheep wandering through heath, gorse, and ferns. The family found a shady spot by a brook, where they set down a basket for a picnic lunch. Norbert showed everyone a crack underneath a big rock.

Gilberte peered in, then stepped back. "It's dark!"

"Yes, beautifully dark, darker than anywhere on Earth," Norbert said.

"We have candles and a lantern," Elisabeth assured her daughter.

"It's yucky. Don't go, Mama!" Gilberte said. "Papa, please stay!"

"Grand-mère will stay with you," Norbert said.

"Let's roll stones into potholes," his mother said. "We can wade in the stream."

"Will you come back, Mama?" Gilberte asked.

Elisabeth took a deep breath of air scented with juniper, moss, and the mint growing by the brook. She knew there was always a chance that even the most cautious person wouldn't come out of a cave. Some people stumbled into an abyss. Shale could crumble under climbers' hands. Some unlucky cavers never found their way back out of winding dark tunnels that were hard to distinguish from others.

"I've been caving for more than ten years. I've always been all right." Elisabeth smoothed Gilberte's hair, which was wavy and brown like hers. "I'll be careful. Now, give me a kiss."

Elisabeth and Norbert couldn't fit through the space under the rocks while wearing knapsacks, so they tied the knapsacks to ropes and dragged them. Elisabeth took a deep breath, gripped a lit candle between her teeth, and wedged herself under the rock. She squirmed along the slimy bottom with her back scraping the rock ceiling. Soon the tunnel widened enough for her to crawl on hands and knees. When her candle flame flickered, Elisabeth paused. Rotting leaves or grass could create a poisonous gas, which could cause a flame to go out. The candle remained lit, so she moved ahead.

The ceiling gradually grew high enough that she and Norbert could crouch, then stoop over and shuffle down twisting corridors. After making a turn, Elisabeth and Norbert took notes or drew sketches to help them find their way back out. Bats fluttered out of their way. Elisabeth held in her elbows and placed her feet with care, to avoid stumbling on loose rocks. They never knew whether the darkness before them hid another safe patch of ground, a wall, or a deep, deep hole.

Soon they could stand. They stepped around stalagmites and under stalactites.

"Look!" Elisabeth pointed to a row of horses, molded from clay, on the wall. She made out the head of an openmouthed lion. A figure that seemed to be a bison looked as if it had been etched into the rock with a sharp stone. Other animals also showed the thoughtful hands of artists from more than twenty thousand years before. The sculptors' footprints were still in the dust.

Elisabeth and Norbert held each other's hands. The delicately drawn lines, made deep in the earth, far from the ordinary world, suggested that long ago this dark place might have been a sanctuary, used for some kind of prayer.

The sky had almost grown dark by the time they returned from the cave. The sleeping girls rested their heads on their grandmother's lap.

Elisabeth threw down her helmet. She was delighted to unbend her back and swing her elbows without worrying that they'd slam into a wall. She flung open her arms and twirled around. "You won't believe what we discovered!" she cried.

"Yes, yes," Norbert's mother said. "I forgot my knitting, and ever since the children began to doze, I've had nothing to do but think about dinner. You can tell me while we walk."

Elisabeth and Norbert sat by the stream to clean their boots with wild mint. A shepherdess leading home a flock of sheep called a greeting. Elisabeth and Norbert each picked up a child to carry home as shadows folded over the valley.

During the following weeks, Elisabeth and Norbert returned to sketch and make maps. Once they stayed in the cave so long that the worried shepherdess called people from the village, who gathered at the cave's entrance to shout their names. Later, reporters and scientists came to take pictures while Elisabeth and Norbert looked for other caves with prehistoric art that might answer questions, and raise new ones, about the first people who lived on Earth.

That same year a hydroelectric company asked Norbert for help finding underwater rivers in the Pyrenees mountains. The company hoped to use the force of water flowing underground to provide power to make electricity.

"Go ahead," Elisabeth told her husband. She was expecting their third child, and her belly was too large to squeeze through slender tunnels.

"We'll go when the baby's born," Norbert said.

Elisabeth smiled. Norbert always felt more anxious about childbirth than he ever did about caving.

Elisabeth encouraged him to go explore the hills near Ariège. She stayed home and spent many days playing peekaboo with Maud, who was then three years old. Elisabeth tried to teach Gilberte to whistle a long, a short, then a long high note, the family's way to signal a safe arrival at the end of a dark tunnel.

Gilberte pursed her lips, but all that came out was one weak sound. "I can't!" She frowned.

"You can't *yet*," her mother said. "Now, want to play hide-and-seek?"

A week passed, and Norbert came home, smiling.

"You found a new way into the mountains!" Elisabeth hugged him.

"With some help from our friends the birds. I saw a jack-daw on a ledge, climbed up, and wiggled into a tunnel that got so narrow I had to chisel my way through. I went as far as I could alone."

"I can't wait to join you there!" Elisabeth said. Entering a new cave felt like opening a present. She gave birth to a baby boy named Raoul. Then about a year passed before she could leave the three children and go to Ariège. She and Norbert climbed the cliffs, squirmed through a tunnel, dropped a long rope down a hole, and shinnied down. They came to another shaft and dropped a rope the length of a six-story building. The rope didn't reach the ground. Elisabeth pulled a newspaper from her knapsack, crumpled it, lit it, and tossed it down the shaft. The flaming paper fluttered down. Its blaze brightened before burning out on the ground. The brief light revealed that the end of the rope dangled close enough to the bottom that they could slide down it and jump.

Norbert drove an iron spike into the rock. Elisabeth tied the rope to the spike and said, "I'll meet you at the bottom." She murmured a quick prayer. The rope swung as she clutched and loosened her hands and legs to slide down. She jumped to the ground and whistled one long note, a short note, then a long high note to let Norbert know she'd arrived safely. He shinnied down.

They waded through a cold stream that had slowly carved the limestone walls around them. The path turned dry and led to a stream of water splashing down vertical rock. They took out flashlights that they'd sealed in jam jars so they would stay dry, and climbed the rock beside the rushing water. They followed a passageway to another waterfall and scaled more rock. The next cascade they reached was about thirty feet high.

"Do you think we can climb it?" Norbert yelled so Elisabeth could hear over the waterfall's roar.

"Let's try," she said. She was about halfway up the cliff beside the cascade when the rock under one of her feet split. Shale crumbled. Elisabeth plunged backward into the pool beneath the waterfall. Water frothed and swirled over her head. She struggled out of the whirlpool, swam to the quieter water near the ledge, and climbed out.

Norbert hurried down.

"I wish it were warmer, but I'm all right," Elisabeth assured him. She poured water from her boots. She tried to wring out her clothes, then took off most of them.

Norbert gave her his shirt and belt. "We'd better turn around," he said, cupping his hands around his mouth so she could hear over the water crashing into the pool.

"Wet clothes are no reason to go back. I won't let one wall defeat me."

She climbed the cliff. They explored more tunnels before turning around, then camped and went home. Elisabeth had scaled eight waterfalls and gone about two miles into the mountain and a thousand feet underground.

During the following years, she explored dozens of other caves, stopping briefly to give birth to her fourth child. She was thirty-five in 1940, when her fifth child was due. One evening she stirred soup, added a pillow to a pile the youngest children had stacked into a tower, put a piece of Maud's puzzle into place, and checked Gilberte's mathematics home-

work. She glanced at the paper Norbert had unscrolled from
the typewriter, then handed him the wooden spoon she was
holding. She rested a hand on her big belly, told her husband
and children she loved them, and wished them good night.
She was going next door to her sister, who would take her to
the village hospital. She said, "Maybe we'll have a baby here
in the morning."

Norbert served the soup, then tucked the younger children in bed. Ten-year-old Gilberte claimed she wasn't tired.
She was the last child to go upstairs. In the morning, she
awoke to sunshine. Thinking she'd be late for school, she
jumped out of bed and ran downstairs, where her grandmother stood by the stove. Scattered puzzle pieces still lay on
the table. The stack of pillows looked as if it were about to
topple.

"Where's Mama?" Gilberte asked.

"Darling, she passed away."

"No!" Gilberte spun around before her grandmother
could say more. She ran back to her room and slammed the
door. Could it be true that the worst thing in the world had
happened while she lay sleeping? How could she live the rest
of her life without her mother?

Maud's puzzle was never finished, but the stacked pillows
were put back in their proper places. Norbert's mother
washed the wooden spoon, stirred a pot of hot chocolate, and
set bread and jam on the table. Norbert brought home the
baby, who cried and cried at first. But over time that changed,
like everything else. Breakfasts were prepared, matching stockings found, hair brushed and braided, and schoolbooks read.
All the children were taught how to tie reliable knots in ropes,

to carry spare candles in a cave, and to always explore with a trusted companion.

In 1950, ten years after Elisabeth died, Norbert asked Gilberte and Maud to go to the ice cave near the top of the Pyrenees Mountains. He said, "Your mother and I always meant to go back."

Gilberte had grown into a young woman, almost twenty years old. She and Maud climbed with their father to a cave, where they spent almost a day shoveling out snow. The next morning they strapped on helmets worn in World War II and entered the cave. They trekked through snow and slush to the smooth-as-glass frozen lake.

"It's just the same here as it was twenty-four years ago," Norbert said. "Time passes slowly underground."

The father and his daughters crossed the ice, dragging ropes and steel-wire ladders. They marveled at the gray-green reflections in glaciers. Maud stood on tiptoe to peer into a hole in a rock wall. She squirmed in. Gilberte and Norbert held flashlights as her head, chest, hips, and thighs disappeared.

Gilberte caught one of Maud's feet. Her father grabbed the other and held on.

"Are you all right?" Gilberte yelled.

"I'm fine," Maud said. "There's a sudden drop. Let me see how far."

Gilberte heard Maud break off a chunk of ice. There was a long silence before the ice struck the bottom after a long, long drop. Gilberte and Norbert tugged Maud back out of the hole.

They trudged through halls filled with snow, then into a

hall brightened by stalagmites, stalactites, and what looked
like bushes with branches of delicate ice flowers. They stopped
at a hole, estimated its depth, and drove a piton into the rock.
They fastened a sixty-foot steel-wire ladder, which dangled a
few feet above the ground.

"Who wants to go after me?" Norbert asked.

"You go, Maud," Gilberte said. "I'll wait up here till I
hear you're safely down."

They laughed. It was a family joke that of all Gilberte's
skills, whistling was not one. Norbert climbed down the
swaying ladder and gave a long high whistle. Maud scrambled
down and whistled, too. Gilberte worked her way down the
ladder, which twirled and twisted with her weight. When she
bumped against the rock walls, she used an elbow to push
herself back.

She leaped to the ground, where her father and Maud
stood with flashlights. They turned down a corridor that
ended in another frozen cascade. They drove in ice picks to
climb the nearly vertical ice.

On their way to a grotto, they passed shimmering stalactites, crystal shrubs, plumes, and columns. Gilberte rubbed
her numb fingers, then pointed her flashlight at the wall. She
stopped breathing as she recognized her mother's handwrit-
ing.

"Hope," Elisabeth Casteret had written many years ago.
"Courage."

Gilberte touched the words scratched on rock.

"Do you want to turn around?" her father asked.

"Not yet," Gilberte said. "Let's see what's ahead."

—

Elisabeth Casteret (1905–1940) made more than three hundred cave expeditions, mostly in her native France but also in Spain and northern Africa. Some of these explorations were chronicled by her husband, Norbert Casteret, in books and National Geographic *articles. After Elisabeth died, other women, including Gilberte and Maud, continued exploring caves to learn about ancient people and how life on Earth evolved.*

HOW MANY SECRETS CAN BE FOUND IN A FOREST?
NICOLE MAXWELL

Nicole Maxwell danced across the stage of the Paris Opéra. At the end of the ballet, she gracefully spread her arms, dipped her knees, and let her perfect curtsy linger. This might be the last applause she'd ever hear, at least from a stage. She'd practiced and performed ballet since she was a girl in San Francisco, California, but she'd begun to think there must be more to life than this wonderful work that left her no time or energy for anything else. She would miss the other ballerinas and her adopted land, but at age twenty-seven, she was ready to find something new and grand to do.

In 1933, she married a U.S. Air Force officer. Nicole and her husband traveled to Hawaii and the Polynesian islands. Nicole studied ritual dances and recorded the many ways women waved their hands and arms to tell stories. In recognition of this work, she was named a Fellow of the Royal Geographical Society. When her husband was sent to military bases in Massachusetts, Ohio, and Washington, D.C., Nicole took college courses and spent a year and a half in medical school. But none of her classes led to work she might pursue with passion, and as twelve years passed, her husband seemed to feel more and more that she was some sort of inconvenient luggage. Every time they moved, he behaved as if she were in the way. Moreover, Nicole's restlessness grew deeper.

She and her husband divorced in 1945, and she moved to New York City. In 1947, she visited friends in Lima, Peru. While she kept her elegant New York apartment, which she'd filled with souvenirs from her days performing in Paris, she liked South America so much that she stayed to become a reporter for the *Lima Times*. She also wrote travel guidebooks in English and Spanish.

Peru's capital was full of fascinating people, but Nicole became increasingly fond of parts of the country that couldn't be reached by road. One day in 1952, she and some native guides were exploring an area of the Amazonian rain forest filled with so many bushes that they had to swing machetes to hack out a path. Nicole ducked under vines and nests that draped from the tallest trees she'd ever seen. Red, pink, and purple petals fell from flowers that grew on the treetops, the only place in the dense forest that received enough sunlight to blossom. Nicole heard the sounds of monkeys chittering, mosquitoes whining, and their machetes' sharp blades splitting branches. Glancing up, she saw parrots, red-eyed tree frogs, and snails clinging to the undersides of enormous leaves. Shaggy sloths hung from branches.

Nicole was thinking it was time to sit down and rest,

when she lost her grip on her machete. It swung into her left arm. She slapped her right hand over the wound, but blood gushed out. She tore off the light shirt she wore as protection from the mosquitoes and wrapped it around her arm. Within seconds, blood soaked through the cloth.

Two guides bent over her, talking anxiously, but the third man grabbed a gourd and dashed into the rain forest. Nicole felt so stunned and dizzy that she wished she might leap after him and perhaps find a doctor standing beneath a palm tree, studying the philodendron vines that curled around its trunk. Her mind cleared, and she knew that running wouldn't solve her problem and that hospitals were hundreds of miles away. She tied another shirt over her deep cut. Her medical training had been enough to reassure her that she wasn't losing a fatal amount of blood, but she didn't have any antibiotics to stop an infection, which could kill her. She didn't want to die here, not before she'd found one great or good thing to do with her life.

The guide who'd raced into the forest returned with a split gourd filled with a thick red liquid. "Drink this," he said. "Now."

Nicole looked down at the blood seeping through her improvised bandage. What did she have to lose? She drank the tree sap. Within a few minutes, her arm stopped bleeding.

She continued through the forest, where brilliant birds darted from tree to tree. Steam rose from the humid ground. Nicole understood that the wonders of the jungle weren't only the wonders she could see. She wanted to learn about the cures hidden there.

That wasn't going to be easy. Her wound healed quickly

and didn't even leave a scar, but when Nicole thanked her guide, he only shrugged. He refused to show her the type of tree where he'd found the sap that had saved her. "These lessons must come from one's mother or father, and their mothers and fathers who lived long ago," he said. "The forest's secrets are not for strangers."

Nicole returned to Lima, where she spoke with anyone she thought might know about healing plants and trees in the rain forests. She spoke with families walking single file down sidewalks, the way they walked on narrow jungle trails. She stopped a man with a snake wrapped around his arm and asked, "Have you heard of a tree with sap that stops bleeding?" She bought ice cream for missionaries and soda for a *guardia* who'd spent years policing the forests. She learned only enough to know how much more there was to learn.

Nicole thought she'd have better luck farther from the cities. She wanted to travel up small rivers and meet people who lived the way their ancestors had, depending on the forests for food and medicine. She needed support to make the long trip she had in mind.

Nicole quit her job at the newspaper and went to New York City to talk with doctors and scientists about the knowledge she knew was hidden in the vast rain forests of the Amazon. Most people laughed at the thought of finding medicine in trees.

"You must remember that aspirin was first found in willow trees," Nicole said. "Malaria killed thousands of people before quinine was discovered in the bark of Peru's cinchona trees. Curare from the rain forests aids in surgery by temporarily numbing nerves. There may be thousands of herbs and trees that haven't been studied. Some might even save lives."

Finally a pharmaceutical company offered enough money for Nicole to spend a year talking with people and getting samples of plants to bring back for scientists to analyze. Nicole got busy packing lentils, rice, oatmeal, coffee, sugar, and powdered milk, as well as her radio and camera. She bought blue jeans and high-top sneakers. Then she raced around the city buying little mirrors, fishhooks, nail polish, beads, and ballpoint pens for gifts in a land where money might not matter. She even bought artificial eyes, which she hoped might dazzle a witch doctor, or shaman, enough to tell her the secret powers of plants.

In 1958, Nicole boarded a ship bound for South America. As it sailed closer to the equator, the weather got warmer. Most passengers swapped woolen scarves for straw hats and lounged on deck chairs. Nicole wanted to strengthen her legs for hiking. She used the ship railing as a ballet barre to practice pliés and battements.

After the ship docked in Lima, Nicole climbed into a small airplane to make a trip of about eight hundred miles over mountains and jungles. The plane rose more than twenty thousand feet to clear the rocky, snow-covered Andes, then flew above forests broken by narrow, twisting rivers. It landed in Iquitos, a major port on the Amazon River. There Nicole got a ride in a dugout canoe to a farm run by old friends. Most of the workers were Witoto Indians, who lived in thatched huts that stood on stilts.

Nicole spent a few weeks talking with people when they weren't working in the banana, orange, and mango groves, or in fields of tall silvery green lemongrass that was exported to make perfume. She painted girls' fingernails red. She clicked open ballpoint pens and drew pictures on their arms. People smiled as she passed out safety pins and sweets. But when Nicole asked, "Have you seen a tree with sap that can stop bleeding?" they closed their mouths tight. Even their eyes got smaller as they shook their heads.

One day Nicole was brushing her long reddish brown hair to help it dry in the sun, when Witoto children and adults came to watch. They touched her hair and tried out her hairbrush on each other.

Since they discussed her looks quite intimately, Nicole thought she could ask a personal question. "I've noticed the older women here have very healthy teeth," she said. "Younger women don't."

Antonio, a farmer who often translated Witotoan into Spanish for her, nodded. "The older people used to chew leaves from the yanamuco tree," he said. "It kept their teeth from decay."

This was exactly the sort of information Nicole had been hoping to find. She spoke Witotoan as she asked two boys to bring yanamuco leaves for her to eat.

Everyone laughed, the way they always did when she spoke their language. The boys dashed into the forest and returned with a branch. As Nicole broke off a leaf and raised it to her mouth, people laughed even harder.

Antonio stopped laughing long enough to say, "No, señora, stop! The leaves will turn your teeth black for a while. The older people didn't mind, but no one does that today."

Nicole chose not to chew the leaves, but she took them to

her room to preserve them with her plant press. She'd carry them home, where scientists might be able to isolate the properties that prevented cavities while eliminating the plant's unpleasant effects.

Of course Nicole wanted to learn much more. Two Witoto Indians agreed to lead her up a tributary of the Amazon River. They filled a dugout canoe with supplies and left at midnight to travel by moonlight and avoid the heat. When these guides turned back, Nicole got a ride on a barge filled with baskets of *leche caspi*, rubbery tree sap that would be sent to a chewing-gum factory in the United States. Sometimes she rode in dugout canoes that had motors, but she preferred paddling, so that she could hear the trill, chatter, and screeches of birds and animals in trees. The dark river hid piranha fish and water snakes such as the anaconda. Nicole breathed the scents of flowers blooming too high above to see.

When the river grew too narrow or swampy for a canoe, Nicole and new guides hiked through the rain forest. When they faced a cliff, they climbed it. When trails were flooded, they slogged through waist-deep water. They sang and whooped to scare off snakes, then grew quiet, listening for jaguars. They watched out for scorpions, tarantulas, poison-ous caterpillars, fire ants, leaf-cutter ants, and ants that bit from the front and stung from the back. Even some trees and plants could sting if they were touched. But Nicole always re-membered that these dangerous forests might hold powerful cures.

Late on most afternoons, she and her guides stopped at the nearest village, where they were always offered a place to hang their hammocks. Nicole handed out strings of beads or flashed little mirrors. Most people were friendly, until she asked, "Can you show me plants that might save lives?"

Nicole didn't learn a thing. She knew that people had gone there to dig gold or cut down trees for rubber to make car tires, so she tried to be patient with the lack of trust.

She kept on traveling up smaller rivers and through thicker forests. She sweated and itched. As she balanced on log bridges, she remembered dancing at the Paris Opéra and couldn't help missing the music and old friends. She didn't like bathing in rivers with an eye out for crocodiles, but she wasn't ready to turn back.

She headed up the Tigre River toward Ecuador. At a Jivaro village, people admired her camera and the songs that hummed from her radio. The face of Rukas, the witch doctor, was painted with red-and-black designs. His trousers were belted with a vine. Rukas looked pleased with the glass eye that Nicole gave him, and he honored her by putting on his feathered headdress. But when she asked about the tree with sap that could stop bleeding, he walked away.

Tesa, the witch doctor's daughter, must have seen that Nicole needed cheering up. She gave Nicole her baby to play with while she did chores around her house without walls. Then Nicole washed pots, and Tesa bounced the baby. Nicole dreaded going back to the scientists with empty hands, so she decided to stay there awhile. Relying on the Spanish words both she and Tesa knew and the gestures Nicole remembered from Polynesian dances, Nicole taught her new friend some English and Tesa taught her the language of the Jivaros. They made meals together. Tesa showed Nicole some traditional dances. Nicole showed her some ballet positions.

Of course, the scientists hadn't paid her to talk, cook, and dance. Nicole was looking for Tesa to say goodbye when she found her friend gathering plants. Before she broke a stem, Tesa nodded to say "thank you." She touched each plant as tenderly as she touched her baby.

"These are for soup, but I know some healing plants," Tesa said. "I can show you where to find them."

"I'm leaving now," Nicole said. "But I'll come back. Maybe you can show me then."

Tesa smiled so broadly that Nicole guessed that none of the strangers who'd stopped there had ever returned. Nicole traveled up the river for a few weeks, then went back to spend more time in the Jivaro village. Tesa showed Nicole leaves and roots used by her mother and grandmothers and great-grandmothers, too. They filled baskets with marsh grass, bulbs, and bark. Tesa talked about her father while digging roots that could cure a stomachache. She spoke about her mother's hands while clipping leaves. She untangled vines and confided dreams she had for her daughter.

Nicole told stories, too, about the places she had been. She pressed plants and took notes. Then it was time to say goodbye again. "I'll come back," she said.

Nicole took her plants and notebooks to the scientists in New York City. She enjoyed hot showers and her soft bed, but she missed washing her face in the dew of a gigantic leaf. She missed swinging in a hammock, hearing the river instead of traffic. Nicole put her bedspreads and china plates in storage. She bought a ticket back to South America.

She had a house built in Peru, far from roads, where she tended an astonishing garden. She often paddled down rivers to see Tesa and meet other people. Some showed her how to make tea from the retama's yellow flowers, which were said to cure fevers. Others taught her to recognize the *indano* tree, the bark and sap of which were used to treat wounds and stomach problems. Nicole learned many ways to treat ailments with leaves, vines, roots, bark, and sap. And finally she stood under the heart-shaped leaves of a *sangre de grado* and cut its smooth bark. A dark red liquid oozed from the tree. It was the same kind of resin that, years before, had stopped the blood flowing from her wounded arm and helped it heal. Nicole had found her miracle tree. She curtsied, thanking the tree that had given her a second chance at life and the continent that had given her a home.

—

Nicole Maxwell (1906–1998) spent the next forty years of her life among thousands of blooming, twisting, and fluttering plants. She collected and made extensive notes about more than 350 plants and trees known to cure excessive bleeding, scars from burns, and skin and eye diseases. Scientists continue to study these specimens along with those collected by others. While vines, bark, roots, leaves, and flowers from all over the world can be and are used for healing, today special attention is paid to those from Central and South America because of the great diversity within the endangered rain forests of these areas.

HOW DEEP CAN WE DIVE?
SYLVIA EARLE

The first time Sylvia Earle stood by the ocean, a wave pulled sand out from under her bare feet. More waves rose and crashed, and one curled over the small girl's head. Sylvia's knees buckled. She fell facedown and couldn't breathe for what seemed like a long time. When the weight of water lessened, she struggled to her knees and grabbed her mother's waiting hand.

"Let's find a towel and dry you off," Mother said as she led Sylvia higher up the beach.

"No!" Sylvia ran back into the water. Her eyes stung. Her mouth puckered from salt. Sand was caught in her bathing suit. Another wave knocked her over and briefly held her down, but Sylvia wouldn't stay onshore.

During the rest of the family's vacation, Sylvia hunted for sea stars, crabs, and shells. She studied these as carefully as she observed violets and frogs when they went home to her family's small New Jersey farm.

"Hold it gently," Mother said when Sylvia caught a bull-frog. Mother wet her hands in the creek and formed her fingers into a cup. She held the frog so that Sylvia could examine its gold-ringed eyes, strong legs, and web feet. "Now we'll put it back where we found it," Mother finally said.

The farm was a wonderful place, but in 1948 Sylvia's family moved to Dunedin, a town near Tampa Bay in Florida. Sylvia called the ocean her blue backyard. She and her two brothers examined tidal pools and swam in the Gulf of Mexico. She watched horseshoe crabs shuttle from sea to shore. Cranes lifted their long, slender legs above the salt marshes. Conchs nestled in the sea grass. Sea urchins crept along the rocks. Sylvia was fascinated by all the life, and when she was twelve years old, she started a collection of sea plants. Often she stayed outside till sunset, when pink-and-orange clouds briefly blazed above the turquoise sea.

In 1952, when Sylvia was sixteen, a friend invited her to dive underwater using equipment that belonged to his father. Sylvia put on a copper helmet with a tube connected to a supply of compressed air. She plunged into the Weeki Wachee River and sank thirty feet to the bottom. As she tried to keep her balance in the current, she saw an alligator slowly open and close its mouth as if to show off its teeth, then slither away in the river rushes. Sylvia started to follow but was distracted by a group of golden brown fish. She stared until she realized they were looking at her, the interloper in their neighborhood. She stayed underwater about twenty minutes, then began to feel dizzy and tugged the hose, signaling her need to go back up. Once back on dry land, she knew her life had changed.

Her mother encouraged Sylvia to learn to type, thinking she'd be more likely to find a job in an office than in the ocean, but when Sylvia chose to major in marine botany at Florida State University, her parents were behind her all the way. Sylvia specialized in the study of algae in the Gulf of Mexico, learning about the plants that provide both food and shelter to many ocean creatures, from microscopic parasites to enormous fish.

She continued her studies at Duke University. She was the only woman in most of her science classes, but she found that if she stayed on the edges of social groups, kept her sense of humor, and was willing to do twice as much work as the men for half as much credit, she did fine. She married, had two children, and settled in a house next door to her parents' old house on Florida's gulf coast. Sylvia scuba-dived whenever she got the chance and learned techniques from Navy divers at a nearby base. Shrimp fishermen let her join them on boats. She browsed through their catch for a wide variety of red, green, and brown algae, which she cataloged.

One day in 1965, Sylvia left her children with her parents and drove just south of Tampa Bay to the Cape Haze Marine Laboratory. She parked and walked past pens posted with signs that said DANGER—SHARKS. The docks were cluttered with wet towels, snorkels, masks, and pails. Sunburned children baited hooks or helped weigh and measure fish. Teenagers hauled in fishnets.

Sylvia entered a laboratory, where notebooks swelled and curled in the humid air. Scientists were bent over microscopes.

A pelican with a bandaged leg waddled past. A small, dark-haired woman wearing a T-shirt and cutoff jeans headed toward her.

Sylvia shook the woman's hand and looked down at her bare feet. "Dr. Clark?"

"Yes, Eugenie Clark, but please call me Genie." She showed Sylvia around the marine laboratory, which she'd founded about ten years before. She explained that she'd given a school lecture, which had been attended by Anne and William Vanderbilt. "Lucky for me, their son, who was ten at the time, was crazy about fish, and they shared his interest," Genie said. The wealthy Vanderbilt family offered Genie a chance to start a marine laboratory.

Genie showed Sylvia tanks with tiger sharks, sandbar sharks, and dusky, lemon, and nurse sharks. The bigger hammerhead and white sharks were kept within fences in the sea.

"We have a lot to learn from sharks," Genie said. "You probably know they've been on Earth about 400 million years, much longer than we humans have been around. In their natural habitat, they rarely get sick. Some doctors dissect sharks to research cures for cancer."

"Dissecting sharks is one thing, but swimming with them is another," Sylvia said. "You're not afraid?"

"I like the word *cautious* more than *fearful*," Genie said. "No one should forget that some species of sharks can kill. But what's interesting is that most don't want to. Sharks investigate what's around them, just the way we do, but they have to use their mouths, since they don't have hands." She went on to explain, "This laboratory is best known for our shark studies, but we want to study all forms of sea life. We could use an expert on marine plants." She pointed to a mound of brown, gold, and red seaweed, mixed with jellyfish, sea snails, urchins, and orange sponges. "It would be great if you could help us sort and label some of these plants."

Sylvia was finishing her Ph.D. at Duke University, but whenever she could, she came by to untangle and label sea plants. In one clump, she found about twenty kinds of algae. She separated the plants from oysters, sea horses, angel-wing shells, mollusks, and purple sea fans. Later she brought along her daughter and son and taught them how to press the plants between pieces of blotting paper.

Visitors were always welcome at the lab, as long as they followed safety rules near the shark pens and were ready to pitch in and help collect specimens, clean fish tanks, or hose down docks. One scientist drove south every summer, his station wagon crowded with his wife, six children, luggage, and any dead raccoon, snake, or turtle he'd spotted by the side of the road and picked up to dissect later. At Cape Haze, his family sprang out of the car, though the air in the laboratory wasn't much sweeter. Science, especially marine biology and botany, tended to be smelly.

Sylvia enjoyed working with someone who believed that scientists can best understand the ocean when they're willing to get wet. While there was much to learn from fish or algae that had been netted or washed to shore, Sylvia and Genie preferred watching living fish and plants. Scuba gear had improved since they'd first gone underwater wearing heavy helmets attached to tubes. Now they breathed compressed air from tanks strapped to their backs as they watched manta rays glide over sponge-encrusted rocks.

Riding a motorboat to diving spots gave the two women a chance to talk, and Sylvia learned that Genie's father had died when she was a baby, so she'd been raised by her mother and grandmother, who'd both emigrated from Japan. When Genie moved with her husband from New York to start the marine laboratory, her mother and stepfather moved, too, to help out with her children and to start Florida's first Japanese restaurant. Genie became known as the "shark lady" for her pioneering work capturing live sharks, keeping them healthy in pens, and teaching them to obey simple commands, such as pressing a target when they wanted food. Her experiments showed that sharks have more intelligence and memory than people had previously thought.

About a year after Sylvia arrived, Genie told her, "I'm thinking about quitting this job."

"But you love it here!" Sylvia said.

"More than anything, but it's time for a change. If I could leave the lab with someone I trusted, I could return to New York for a while and consider teaching at a university. Sylvia, would you be the resident director?"

Sylvia heard gulls calling, waves lapping the shore, and wind rustling through palm trees. She admired the way Genie balanced marriage, raising four children she'd taught to swim before they could walk, and a deep dedication to science. Sylvia's marriage was in trouble, but she hoped this new job would improve her life.

"It would be an honor to direct the lab," Sylvia said. Then she asked, "What will you do until you go to New York?"

"Travel. My kids should see their father's first home in Greece. And I've been invited by the Crown Prince to visit Japan. I'm taking him a gift."

"A shark?" Sylvia raised her eyebrows.

"A small one. It's a long airplane ride, but we'll stop in Hawaii, where I've arranged to take the shark to the aquarium for a stretch between flights."

Sylvia enjoyed her work at the Cape Haze Marine Laboratory, but the study of sharks remained its focus, and she was more interested in sea plants and other animals. After a year, she left the laboratory in the good hands of another scientist. She divorced, remarried, and moved to Massachusetts, where she did research at Harvard University and the Radcliffe Institute.

After giving birth to her third child, Sylvia became even busier but found it impossible to ignore a notice posted on the bulletin board at Harvard's Museum of Comparative Zoology. Scientists were being sought to spend two weeks in an underwater habitat. Sylvia wrote a proposal, then waited to hear.

When the project manager called, he sounded embarrassed. "There are concerns about men and women living together in one small space," he said. "Not only you, but other highly qualified women have proposed first-rate projects." He took a long breath, then added, "What would you think about leading a team of just women?"

"Why not?" Sylvia said.

The Boston Globe published a front-page story with the headline "Beacon Hill Housewife to Lead Team of Female Aquanauts." Sylvia wondered when she might read a headline such as "Beacon Hill Husband Leads Team of Male Aquahunks," but she just shook her head and got on with her work. At least the ocean was getting some attention.

In July 1970, Sylvia dropped off her children with their

grandparents for a Florida vacation, then headed to the Virgin Islands. She and four other scientists descended to a module fifty feet below the surface, where the sea turned emerald green, then deep blue. Cables connected the module to shore and brought them air, water, and power. The Tektite II module had bunk beds, a hot shower, a television, and a refrigerator stocked with frozen dinners. Sylvia and her colleagues stayed in the water as much as possible, returning to the module to recharge their air tanks, change the batteries in their cameras, eat, and sleep.

As fish swam by the Tektite II again and again, Sylvia started to recognize some of them. She noticed the two scratches in one angelfish's fin. The fish seemed to accept the module, which had become part of their landscape. Sylvia watched the way they met or passed one another, gliding over undersea cliffs and coral canyons. A long, slim barracuda swished by. Red, yellow, and blue fish darted around sea fans. Snails crawled and crabs scuttled across sand. Parrot fish nibbled algae.

Witnessing twenty-four-hour cycles undersea let Sylvia note the differences between night creatures and those that swam by day. She woke at dawn and heard the grunts of groupers and the clicking sounds of shrimp. When basket starfish curled up to rest, cardinal fish and squirrelfish began their days. Sylvia became familiar with five gray angelfish who were among the first up and out of the crevice where they'd spent the night. Parrot fish wiggled out of the clear cocoons they'd spun to sleep in. Triggerfish slipped out of the sand, which shifted with the tides.

At dusk, many creatures crept, swam, slithered, or burrowed under shells, rocks, or sand. As moon- and starlight pooled on the sea's surface, fish with big eyes, such as sweepers, came out of hiding. Sea urchins searched for algae. Coral polyps stretched their tentacles to catch plankton. Sylvia did backflips and somersaults, just for fun, which left a trail of sparkles from planktonic species hardly visible during the day.

At the end of two weeks, Sylvia and the other four women left the underwater lab. They were greeted with cheers and bouquets of roses, and driven in a limo leading a ticker-tape parade. Reporters asked, "Were you scared? Did you eat fish? Did you and the other women quarrel?" Sylvia gave short answers: she was generally more scared walking through a dark parking lot at night than she was undersea; they'd microwaved fish sticks from their freezer; and they had enjoyed one another's company. She tried to turn the conversation to what she'd found: 35 kinds of plant-eating fish and 154 varieties of plants, including 26 species never before identified in the Virgin Islands.

The publicity brought Sylvia a chance to travel around the world, talking about wonders that couldn't be seen from ships or shore. She met Katy and Roger Payne, scientists who'd spent about ten years recording whale sounds with underwater microphones. "We just wish we could know what whales look like when they're singing underwater," Katy Payne said. "We can't see that deep."

"You need someone to watch them from underwater," Sylvia said. "I'll go."

In February 1977, she crouched in a small boat several miles off Maui, a Hawaiian island. The rubber boat bobbed in the waves. Swimming with whales had seemed like a good idea onshore, but as Sylvia dipped a flipper in the water, it was hard not to think about what would happen if a creature the size of a truck bumped into her. Humpback whales were known to be friendly, but they weighed eight hundred times what she did.

Sylvia waved at the people on the nearby ship and jumped.

A pregnant whale swam straight toward her.

Turn around, Sylvia thought. *Please turn around.* She couldn't swim fast enough to get out of the way.

The forty-ton whale swam almost close enough to touch. Then, with a lift of a flipper, a swish of her tail fluke, the whale swerved around Sylvia. The creature's long back arced as she rose to the surface, exhaled, and dived back in, smacking the water's surface with flukes and fins.

Sylvia's fear turned to awe at the grace of that enormous body. She spent a few hours swimming with the whales as they trilled, warbled, sighed, and groaned. She reported what she saw then and during much of the next three months. She noted the marks on the whales' fins, which are as unique to each whale as a thumbprint is to a human. Sylvia and the other scientists found out that some of the whales they'd seen in Hawaii, where the creatures mated and had babies, spent summers in the colder waters near Alaska, feeding on krill. They discovered that whales off the shores of Mexico sang the same songs as whales near Hawaii, three thousand miles away.

After studying migrating whales in oceans near South America, India, and China, Sylvia grew curious about what these "gentle giants" found in depths greater than those she'd ever explored. She investigated ways for humans to dive deeper.

In 1979, having separated from her second husband, Sylvia left her children with their grandparents and tried on a metal diving suit, called the *Jim* after the first person who'd tested an early version. The Jim had been designed for underwater salvage work. It was fitted with a breathing system and would protect a diver from the weight of water above it. The metal suit weighed a thousand pounds on land, but it would be much lighter underwater.

Sylvia was the first scientist to use this diving suit, which had been designed for big, muscular men. Lifts were put inside the metal boots, but she still had to stand on tiptoe and stretch one arm, pulling up the other, to operate the mechanical claws. At least it was convenient to pull her arm out of the sleeve to take notes or scratch her nose. There was plenty of room for a camera, notebook, pencils, an apple, and a chocolate bar.

A ship took Sylvia six miles from Oahu, Hawaii. A submersible carrying a photographer started to take Sylvia down. They came back up twice because wires within the Jim suit she wore had snapped. The wires were fixed, and everything was checked and checked again. But several people told Sylvia, "You shouldn't go down. It's too deep. It's too dangerous."

"I'll be careful," she promised them. She was glad that neither her parents nor her children knew exactly where she was right then.

Once again, she climbed back into the bulky suit, which

was attached to the sub, and descended. She watched the water darken from pale blue to deep blue to almost black. On the bottom of the sea, she pushed a lever to detach her suit from the sub. Without the usual tether to connect a deep-sea diver to the water's surface, she could freely walk on the ocean floor. Only a communication line connected her to the vessel, which cast enough light for her to admire a green-eyed shark and red crabs skittering over pink coral. Seven spiny rays swam over clumps of sponges. Blue lights glowed from a lantern fish. An eel twined around gold coral. Sylvia felt honored to walk where no human had walked before.

Her 1,250-foot descent set a record for a solo dive made without a tether to the ocean's surface. The two and a half hours undersea inspired Sylvia to spend much of the next twenty years working with engineers to design and test submersibles to take people deeper. In 1985, she dived three thousand feet in the Pacific Ocean.

Sylvia married again and divorced for a third time. What remained constant was her love of the ocean. She continued the work she'd begun when she was twelve years old, cataloging plants she found behind her parents' house on the Florida shore. She added more information to her notes about thousands of marine plants, and enjoyed the company of her mother, who was living alone after Sylvia's father had died.

The woman who'd once shown Sylvia how to look closely at frogs and violets now encouraged neighborhood children to notice the wonders outside their doors. Sylvia's mother cared for birds she found onshore, raising orphaned egrets and rescuing an osprey that had been tangled in discarded fishing line. She waved goodbye as her daughter strapped on flippers, pulled on a face mask, and waded into the sea. "Be careful!" she called.

"Of course!" Sylvia said. She swam out, to explore the world one small part at a time.

—

Dr. Sylvia Earle (1935–) has spent more than six thousand hours in the sea. In 1990, the woman Time *magazine called "Her Deepness" became the first woman to be named chief scientist for the National Oceanic and Atmospheric Administration. She helped create national marine sanctuaries, where coral reefs and the water are protected from pollution and overfishing, but she stopped working for NOAA because she thought she could speak more effectively for the ocean as a citizen than as a government representative. In 1998, Sylvia Earle was named an explorer-in-residence at the National Geographic Society.*

Katy Payne (1937–) spent fifteen years studying whales with her husband, Roger Payne. In 1984, soon after the couple separated and their youngest child started college, Katy discovered that elephants could hear sounds that are inaudible to humans. She devoted most of the next twenty years to researching elephants in Africa and India. She learned a lot about how elephants and other animals communicate with low-frequency sounds and today is working with two colleagues to make an elephant dictionary.

Dr. Eugenie Clark (1922–) never gets into a car or airplane without first packing a bathing suit. Popularly known as the "shark lady," she has written books and scientific arti-

cles, won many medals and awards, made thousands of dives, and led dozens of deep-sea expeditions around the world. She has swum with and studied thousands of sharks and discovered eleven new species of fish. To help save the coral reefs of the Red Sea from damage caused by increasing numbers of boats and too much fishing, she helped start Egypt's first national park. Like Sylvia Earle, she continues exploring the sea, which makes up about two-thirds of Earth yet remains filled with mystery.

HOW HIGH CAN WE CLIMB?
JUNKO TABEI

Junko Tabei was ten years old in the spring of 1949, when her teacher announced a trip to hike up a mountain near her home in northern Japan.

"I don't want to go," Junko complained to her mother. "Gym class is bad enough!" She couldn't stand all those balls, bats, nets, hoops, and kids who teased her for being short and weak.

"You can climb Mount Nasu if you want to," her mother said. "Just remember your will and your power."

"But I don't want to climb a mountain!" Junko protested. Her mother had already turned her attention to one of Junko's four older sisters, and Junko knew that her mother's will-and-power talk meant she wouldn't let her stay home.

They drove to the mountain's base. "Just take your time," a teacher said.

That wasn't advice Junko had ever heard in gym class, where everything was a contest, so she felt hopeful. Maybe this wouldn't be just one more opportunity to embarrass herself. Some of her classmates raced up and down the slopes and rocks, but as they climbed higher, they ran out of breath and lagged behind. Some were scared by the high cliffs. Junko kept climbing. Although she'd fumbled balls with her small hands, she firmly grasped the rock. She'd lost races run on her short legs, but her arms were just the right size to haul up her light body. Finally Junko stood at the top. Far below were the classmates who'd picked her last for teams. She felt very, very tall.

After Junko returned from the trip, she started urging her family to spend weekends on mountains. She continued climbing through her teens. When she reached her full height, Junko stood four feet nine inches tall. Many of her friends still looked over her head, but nobody teased her now.

Junko went to college and earned a degree in English literature from Showa Women's University in 1962. She married a man she had met while climbing, and found a job as a teacher. It was fun to pass out books and hear them thump onto desk after desk, but only a few students who opened them saw what she saw: the variety of lives that might be lived, a world beyond the pages waiting to be explored. As soon as it was warm enough to open windows, Junko began daydreaming about summer vacation, which she spent climbing mountains all over Japan. One year she and her husband went to Europe and summited the Matterhorn in the Alps.

Every mountain Junko climbed made her want to climb a higher one. She enjoyed hiking and camping with her husband or groups of men and women, but on high mountains a leader was chosen to make the final decisions about which paths were safe or whether strong winds and dark clouds were signs to turn around. When Junko was the leader, some men grumbled about her choices. When a man was the leader, Junko found she was often assigned more than her share of the cooking and other chores.

"Let's start a women's climbing group," she suggested to some friends.

In 1970, Junko left her job and traveled with the Ladies Climbing Club of Japan to the Himalayas, which boasted many of the world's highest mountains. The women determined paths and set timetables, but they hired Sherpas, men who lived near the mountains of Nepal, as guides and porters to help carry tents, food, and other supplies they'd need for about two months of climbing and camping.

Junko Tabei and her friend Hiroko Hirakawa reached the top of Annapurna, one of the world's most dangerous mountains. They witnessed but were unharmed by the avalanches that were common there. Another year, Junko returned to Nepal to climb Cho Oyu, the sixth-highest peak in the world. From the top she saw Mount Everest. No woman had yet climbed to its summit, which at about twenty-nine thousand feet, or almost five and a half miles, is the highest in the world.

Back in the Tokyo suburbs, Junko told her husband about her view of Mount Everest. She gave birth to their first child and studied maps and books about the Himalayas when the baby was taking naps.

In 1975, Junko Tabei and Eiko Hisano were chosen to co-lead a group of fifteen women up Mount Everest. Eiko was small and strong, like Junko, and, at thirty-four, just two years younger.

"What do you tell people who say women should stay out of dangerous places?" a reporter asked.

"Men have climbed Mount Everest. Why shouldn't we?" Junko glared as if he'd suggested she should spend her days in a kimono, arranging flowers or serving tea in fragile cups.

"They say that for every four or five people who have reached the peak of Everest, at least one person has died," the reporter said.

"I know the odds are brutal." Junko had done her research. "I've weighed the chances, and I'm someone who likes to say yes more than no."

"Don't you worry about your little girl?"

"My husband will take good care of her while I'm gone," Junko said. "And my daughter will grow up to know what a woman can do."

In spring, Junko and the climbing team flew to Kathmandu, the busy capital of Nepal. Narrow streets were crowded with women in colorful skirts and shawls, dark-haired men wearing beads over loose shirts, teenage boys wheeling bicycles, and children chasing skinny dogs. From here they would spend a few weeks hiking past villages and through forests to the place where the mountain got snowy and steep. Junko hired forty-five Sherpas to help load tents, food, stoves, ropes, and aluminum ladders onto yaks.

Wearing backpacks stuffed with clothing for the subzero-degree weather on the mountaintop, they passed farmers planting fields of buckwheat, barley, and wheat. Women knit as they walked with their backs bent under the weight of firewood. Wild goats wandered around yellow fields of mustard plants. Butterflies fluttered around pink rhododendrons.

Late every afternoon, the climbers set up tents. The women camped at a little distance from the Sherpas. Junko, Eiko, and their friends heated up packaged soups, ramen noodles, and freeze-dried peas and chicken. Junko heard Ang Tshering Sherpa, one of the leaders, laugh while the Sherpas cooked curried rice and lentils and drank sour yak milk or mugs of sweet tea. Every morning the team climbed higher, passing tea shops and monasteries, where monkeys scrambled over stone statues of the Buddha.

They spent one night in a village, where some women glanced at Junko and Eiko, then looked away when they smiled. Junko wondered if they were curious or disapproving. Did they ever think about what the view might be like from the top of the mountain? She watched two girls run through an apple orchard, where branches frothed with pink-and-white blossoms. One girl glanced over her shoulder, looked Junko in the eye, then pulled herself up onto the boughs.

"Climb," Junko said, though the girl was too far away to hear. "Climb high."

Day after day, the Japanese women and the Sherpas hiked over hills made bright by bluebells, lilies, ferns, and thistles. They balanced on narrow, swaying bridges to cross rivers. They trekked past waterfalls, bamboo thickets, and wild mango and lotus trees. After they reached pine and juniper forests, the route became chillier and steeper. Villages became smaller and farther apart, until there were no houses at all.

They passed a temple where Buddhist monks with shaved heads and red robes walked in well-kept gardens. Beyond the monastery were slopes where no one lived.

When they reached the part of the mountain that was too cold and rocky for trees to grow on, Junko's backpack felt heavier. She looked at Mount Everest's great pointed peak. Plumes of snow blew on winds that sometimes moved as fast as 150 miles per hour. Her heart beat faster because of both the altitude and her desire to climb.

"The English named the mountain after an early surveyor," Ang Tshering said. "We have always called her Chomolungma to honor the goddess who lives on top, the mother goddess of the world."

Junko liked that name.

Every day now, the world looked more white and blue with snow, sky, and clouds. Junko heard avalanches rumble and looked up to see massive waves of snow slide and billow over ice, pulling along more snow. From time to time, the climbers passed piles of rocks that marked places where others had died. Junko and Eiko glanced at each other after seeing those rocks but didn't speak.

They set up their tents near a frozen river that had broken up over thousands of years, leaving huge chunks of ice that had never entirely melted. Some ice formations were taller than houses and as wide as city blocks. All looked thrown together and piled every which way, as if by a mad giant. Even small changes in temperature could make the ice melt just enough to shift. Towers of ice might topple. Ice could split open, making deep crevasses. The ice under a climber's feet could collapse without warning.

Ang Tshering and the other Sherpas strung up prayer flags, squares of orange, blue, and green cloth, which they hoped would carry their prayers for a safe journey up the mountain. They lit juniper branches and chanted. They tossed blessed rice and barley flour, then rubbed the pale flour left on their hands in each other's hair, praying that they should all live to be gray-haired.

On the day they would start scaling the Khumbu Ice Falls, all the climbers got ready to leave at dawn. They did not want to be on the ice when the late afternoon sunlight was likeliest to cause melting. Junko strapped crampons onto her boots. She hoped the spikes on the soles would keep her from slipping. She checked in with Eiko. "Are you okay?"

"Never been better." Eiko's dark eyes glistened behind her wire-framed glasses.

They slipped ropes through carabiners and clipped themselves together. They made their way above and between clear, white, and blue-green glaciers that had broken, tumbled, and cracked. They swung ice axes into vertical ice walls, which they climbed. When they faced wide crevasses, Junko and the others made aluminum ladders into bridges by laying them horizontally from one side to the other. They balanced carefully as they walked across these ladders suspended over hundreds of feet of air.

The fifteen women and forty-five Sherpas made it up nearly two thousand feet of ice.

With much thanksgiving, they set up a new camp, where they would spend a week or two letting their bodies get used to the thinner air. The Sherpas' prayer flags and the women's parkas made bright spots among blue-and-white snow, ice, clouds, and sky. Almost everyone had headaches from the low oxygen. Many were coughing, and others couldn't keep down even a small meal. They had to be more and more careful that headaches and nausea didn't worsen into altitude sickness or edema, a disease in which leakage of fluids in the brain or lungs could become severe enough to cause death. Junko often hiked with Eiko; they watched gales blow snow from the mountain-top and talked about the clouds. Cumulus clouds were reassuring: their fluffy contours usually meant good weather; but long, wispy cirrus clouds frequently forecast storms.

Some members of the group decided to stay at this camp, but others climbed higher. They were fixing dinner when Junko heard the crack, roar, and rumble of plummeting snow.

"Avalanche!" Eiko yelled. "Run for your life!" The wind swept away her words.

Junko grabbed her ice ax, ran from her tent, and saw sheets of snow and ice cascading faster than cars speeding on a highway. She crouched and slammed down her ice ax to keep the swift sheets of snow from pushing her down the slope. She flung an arm over her mouth and nose so she wouldn't breathe ice.

The world turned dark as snow buried her. The small space she'd made between her arm and nose gave her some air to breathe. She heard Sherpas chanting prayers while they frantically dug and pushed aside snow.

Junko slowly lifted her arms. Snow fell off her jacket when the men helped her up. Standing on unsteady legs, gasping for air, she whispered, "Is everyone all right? Is everyone alive?"

Before she heard an answer, Junko sank to the ground. She was carried to shelter, where her companions rigged up a sort of oxygen tent. As her mind cleared, she learned that the Sherpas, whose tents had been just far enough from the women's to have remained uncovered, had managed to dig out every woman who'd been buried under snow. Everyone survived. Junko heard women digging out tents and sleeping bags, or picking up scattered knapsacks, stoves, and pans. Others rubbed each other's hands and feet, which gradually turned from white to healthier shades of pink and beige and tan. Junko mended her broken glasses with rubber bands.

"Thank you," Junko told the Sherpas. "Thank you for saving our lives."

"It is our job," Ang Tshering said simply.

During the following days, Junko doled out aspirin. Her face was so sore that she could hardly lift her chin or open her eyes wide enough to look at the peak. It was as beautiful as ever, but Junko had to wonder if Chomolungma, mother goddess of the world, was telling them to turn back.

"Junko." Eiko put her hand on her friend's arm. The skin around her eyes was swollen and a faint shade of purple. She said, "I'm not going any farther."

Junko nodded. She meant her silence to suggest that no explanation was needed, but Eiko continued. She said, "It's not just the avalanche that's rattled me. My headaches have been getting worse. I can hardly think."

Junko nodded again. Of all the effects of extreme altitudes, the way the thin air could harm a person's judgment frightened her the most. She knew of a climber whose concentration failed just long enough so that she slipped off her gloves to tie her shoe, and by the time she'd straightened her back, her fingers had turned black with frostbite. Even worse, some climbers had headed straight into terrible storms.

"Maybe we should all turn around," Junko said.

"No! Junko, you must reach the peak," Eiko said. "It will be a triumph for all of us."

Most of the others in the group also decided to stay in the camp, and twelve days after the avalanche some got ready to set out again. Junko slathered her face with sunscreen. She dressed in thermal underwear, waterproof pants, polypropylene socks, high-tech boots, a down jacket, and sunglasses to protect her eyes from the glare of sun on snow. Junko and four other women and five Sherpas made their way up the steep, icy slopes. Their crampons squeaked as they walked along the edge of a crevasse so deep that they couldn't see the bottom.

They roped themselves together to climb a steep, snowy slope. Anyone taking a step back would find his or her foot resting on nothing but air, and might drop hundreds of feet. One stumble on loose rock or ice could mean several deaths.

The climbers set up another camp, one long day's climb from the peak. When the weather cleared, Ang Tshering agreed to go up with Junko for this final, most hazardous climb. On May 16, 1975, they awoke just before sunrise so they'd have as much light as possible to reach the peak and return before dusk. Junko put on her warmest clothes. She packed snacks, water, and bottled oxygen to use near the summit, where there was about one-third less oxygen than at sea level.

Junko's heart beat hard. Even with dark glasses, her eyes

stung from the sunlight glinting off the snow. Her throat felt dry and sore, as if she'd run a long race. Just turning her head or lifting her arm was an effort, but over and over she raised her ice ax and slammed it down to test the depth of the snow or to hold her to icy slopes. Junko lifted one foot after the other. Each foot felt as if it weighed about fifty pounds. "I want to sit down," she yelled over the wind.

"No," Ang Tshering said.

"I have to rest! Just for a minute!"

"No, not even for a minute."

She knew Ang Tshering was right. She'd heard about climbers who sat down and never got up, having lost the energy, the desire, or the ability to think clearly. Junko thought about her mother: "Remember your will and your power." She kept pushing against the mighty, invisible wind.

When they reached a ridge with a sheer drop on both sides, Junko and Ang Tshering clipped their belts to a rope and climbed. They made it to the top of the ridge, then scaled a rock face. Their fingertips, sheathed in thick gloves, gripped cracks in the steep surface. Their feet were protected by boots, but they clenched their toes, using every small and large muscle to hold on. They trudged through the snow to what Junko thought was Everest's peak but turned out to be another ridge. They climbed over it. Breathing bottled oxygen, Junko crawled on hands and knees.

At last, Junko Tabei stood higher than anyone else in the world. The first woman to reach the summit of Mount Everest looked down at where her friends were waiting, anxious and wondering exactly where she was. Farther down, the monks in red robes must be chanting. Women would be carrying kindling on their strong backs, and children racing around trees that might be turning green. All Junko could see was snow and sky.

"Let's go," she said. It was too cold and windy to say much more. Besides, she liked moving more than standing still, even on top of the world. Junko set her mouth in concentration as she and Ang Tshering took small, careful steps. She knew that more people had died going down this mountain than climbing up.

Their strength, concentration, luck, and determination held. The sky remained blue and clear. Junko and Ang Tshering returned to the tents high on the mountain. Triumphantly Junko raised her ice ax and grinned.

After a few days of rest and celebration, they left to meet Eiko and the other women who'd stayed in the camp where they'd experienced the avalanche. They all hiked to the fir forests, then to the valleys they'd left weeks before. Spring had turned to summer while they were gone. Wheat, rice, and barley fields were green with ripening grain. The delicate blossoms of apple and almond trees had fallen. Boughs were brimming with green leaves and small, growing fruits and nuts.

As they entered a village, the women and Sherpas called, "Junko Tabei reached the top!"

Kicking up dust as they ran in bare feet, girls stopped to stare. Goats nibbled the hems of their red and purple skirts. Men dropped hoes in potato fields to look. Women who'd peeked from doorways when the climbers were on their way up now left their houses.

They crowded around Junko and pushed forward with

baskets of apples, too many to eat. Junko didn't speak their language, but as they thrust the baskets toward her, she knew they were saying, "Take. Please take more."

Junko took an apple. Its smooth skin felt good on her dry, rough hands. She bit into the red-and-yellow fruit and let the sweet juice fill her mouth. Nothing had ever tasted so delicious.

"Take more. Please," Junko repeated their words.

The women laughed at hearing her speak their language. Everyone looked at the mountaintop, where fierce winds blew plumes of snow. They could go anywhere. The world felt bigger to them all.

—

In the years following her ascent of Mount Everest, Junko Tabei (1939–) traveled around the world. In 1992, she became the first woman to have reached the summits of the highest mountains of North America, South America, Europe, Africa, Australia, and Antarctica, as well as Asia. Once she'd reached the highest peaks on all seven continents, her next goal became to climb the highest mountain of every country in the world.

Junko has summited more than ninety major peaks in sixty countries. During her years of climbing, she's seen the mountains become increasingly crowded, and too many climbers have left garbage or damaged the land. She became director of the Himalayan Adventure Trust, an agency founded to help protect and clean up mountain environments around the globe. Many trees have been cut for timber in the Himalayan valleys, causing hunger from the loss of fruits and nuts, as well as from farmlands damaged by land erosion. Re-membering the gifts she was given after first climbing Mount Everest, Junko brought young trees to replace those that were cut down. She joined people from the villages in digging holes and planting rows of apple trees.

HOW FAR CAN WE SAIL ALONE?
KAY COTTEE

Kay Cottee sat at the kitchen table with her best friend. The two women were eating cookies and sipping tea, when Kay said, "Ever since I was a little girl, I've wanted to sail around the world. Alone. Without stepping onshore. Don't you think it's time I tried?"

Fredo dropped her cup of tea.

"It's not that surprising, is it?" Kay said while cleaning up the mess. "I was two weeks old the first time my mum and dad took me sailing." As Kay got older, her family continued to spend many weekends on the bay near their home in Sydney, Australia.

Kay finished high school in 1970 and went on to secretarial college. She didn't care much for typing or for working as a seamstress, like her mother. She liked measuring wood and fiberglass more than cloth. She switched to her father's profession of building boats.

"What does Ian think about your round-the-world idea?" Fredo asked.

"I haven't told him yet," Kay said.

"You've been together for ten years!"

"We've been fighting lately. I want to have a baby and he doesn't."

"Sailing alone around the world isn't the usual way to get pregnant."

"I'm almost thirty-three," Kay said. "Sometimes I think I shouldn't stick with a guy who doesn't want kids, but I can't quite face the thought of breaking up. Maybe we could use some time apart."

"Whatever you decide, I'll stand behind you one hundred percent," Fredo said.

Kay worked up the nerve to tell Ian about her dream. Once he'd made sure she had considered all the possible hazards, he said, "Go for it." She was glad to have his support, though she wouldn't have minded if he'd moaned a bit about how much he would miss her.

Finally Kay had to tell her parents. They talked for three hours.

"You're a great sailor, but you know there's a lot you can't predict at sea," her father said.

"What if you get sick?" her mother asked. "No one will be there to help if you break an arm or leg."

"I'll pack a medical kit with antibiotics, bandages, splints, and whatever the doctor suggests." Kay hoped they didn't recall the voyage on which she'd broken a tooth, leaving painfully exposed nerves. She'd rummaged through her tool-box for epoxy pipe-jointing compound, dabbed that on the broken tooth, then sucked mints to cope with the nasty taste.

"Won't you get lonely?" her mother asked.

Kay nodded. She was probably more afraid of the solitude than of anything else.

"If you're certain this is what you want, we'll help you in every way we can," her father said.

Soon Kay bought a hull and deck, which were set on the lawn in front of her apartment. She and her friends spent weeks fixing pumps and installing an engine, a mast, a spar, and sheets. They put extra fiberglass on the hull to make it stronger in case the boat hit something submerged. Kay's father installed electrical wiring. Her mother sewed cushions and painted the walls. Friends helped put in a self-steering instrument so that the sloop could keep sailing while Kay slept. They taught her how to repair electronic equipment such as the two-way radio she'd use to keep in touch with her family and check on weather reports.

Kay designed sails of many shapes and sizes so she'd have a variety of mainsails, spinnakers, headsails, and storm jibs to choose from, depending on the wind's force and direction. She made room for a large sail-repair kit with spare cloth, needles, thread, leather, cord, and pliers.

Of course, these preparations took money. Kay earned some by teaching sailing and working on other people's boats, and she went through her savings fast. She sold almost everything she owned, including her car, then bought a bicycle to get around. She hoped to raise money from a company that wanted the publicity her voyage could bring it. Kay borrowed a classy outfit and a car to meet one potential sponsor at the airport, then got lost driving him to his hotel. While getting out of the car, she caught her high heel in the hem of the skirt and fell flat, spilling everything from her overstuffed briefcase. She didn't impress this man with her navigational skills or her grace. Finally she met the director of Blackmores health-care products, who agreed to sponsor her trip to raise funds for educational programs. To show her gratitude, Kay christened her boat *Blackmores First Lady*.

Kay studied pilot charts and maps with information on winds and currents. She had to pack every last thing she might need, but anything she brought aboard made the ship heavier. No matter how she juggled, there simply wasn't a lot of room. Her mother bought cans of food. Since the labels were likely to get damp, fall off, and make a mess, she peeled them off, wrote the contents on the cans with a waterproof pen, then varnished the cans so they wouldn't rust. Kay would have to wake up about every half hour to check her course, so Fredo went to at least ten stores to test alarm clocks, then bought the loudest. Another friend attached a flashlight to a headband so that Kay could see to work with both hands at night. Her sisters supplied her with six months' worth of books, crossword puzzles, audiotapes, yarn, and chocolate.

Kay didn't expect to sail near ships flying flags with skulls and crossbones, but she worried about modern pirates, mostly drug smugglers, who might be tempted to hijack a boat with only one woman aboard. She took a self-defense course and learned to load, maintain, and shoot her father's rifle.

At last it was time to fill the water and fuel tanks. Kay had prepared for everything except saying goodbye.

"We hope you make it around the world, but we'll love you just as much if you don't." Kay's father glanced at the two-way radio. "If you're in danger, or exhausted, be sure to call for help."

"Lots of things can happen, Dad. But I'm lucky. And I've been taught by the best." Kay hugged her parents.

On November 29, 1987, Kay Cottee set out in her thirty-seven-foot-long sloop. Her parents, her sisters, her friends, and Ian waved from dinghies and small yachts. Kay stood by the railing around her deck, smiling until her face hurt. Although other women had sailed alone around the world, Kay wanted to be the first woman to make the voyage unassisted and without touching shore, which meant she couldn't sail into a port for even one minute. If she wanted to set a record, no one could toss her a package of fresh food or a spare part. She'd be on her own crossing about twenty thousand miles of sea.

Kay waved again, then leaped to the wheel to steer out of the way of a boat. Then she pulled up the jib, spread the mainsail, and left Sydney harbor. She headed toward New Zealand to sail around its southern cape.

In the centuries since Jeanne Baret had disguised herself as a boy to board a ship, sea travel had been made easier, safer, and generally more pleasant by inventions such as two-way radios and generators, which provided electricity for computers and other navigation aids. Vitamin C was now known to prevent scurvy. But the sea itself remained wildly unpredictable. In storms, waves could tower over a sloop's masts and even toss the vessel upside down. Icebergs made voyages near polar seas dangerous. These hazards would be greater for a small boat, especially with just one person to navigate it and keep everything in repair.

Once she was on course, Kay went below to the cabin, where her kitchen, bedroom, and parlor were one cozy room. Books and gear were strapped onto shelves so they wouldn't topple in rough weather. Her old teddy bear was propped on the bunk bed attached to the wall. Nets were strung around to hold her clothes. Snapshots of family and friends were taped everywhere, and Kay found notes and little gifts that they had hidden.

What am I doing? she thought. *Why on earth am I heading away from all the people I love?* She cried.

The wind changed direction. Kay ran up to the deck to steer, and to take down sails and raise new ones. She knew from experience how to choose the sails that would enable the wind to pull her sloop without dragging it too fast. Over the next few days, she spent lots of time watching for tugboats, liners, and tankers, as well as floating garbage, discarded barrels, and logs. Already her sunburned arms were getting stronger.

On her fourth day out, clouds filled more and more of the southern sky. Kay put two reefs in the mainsail and furled the headsail. Huge waves foamed, curled, and crashed. The slanting deck became a slippery slide. Kay clipped on the safety harness before changing sails, which she did eleven times in a few hours, trying to catch winds to keep moving without making her craft glide dangerously fast.

She sailed south of New Zealand and headed toward

South America. As the weeks passed, she spent less time wondering what everyone was doing back home, and more time focused on the wind and sea around her. She chatted with birds and watched dolphins leap, dive, and flip. They raised smooth gray faces as they snorted, whistled, cooed, and trilled. At night, Kay watched the stars and the phosphorescent glow on the waves. Every day she felt a little less lonely than she had the day before. By the end of the first month, she had come to understand that hers was a chosen solitude, not one that had been forced upon her. There was peace in that.

She ran out of fresh fruits, vegetables, and cheese, and relied on food from cans. She got used to the rhythms of the Pacific Ocean and to the increasingly colder air. At night, she left on the kerosene lanterns so she wouldn't bump into dark walls when she got up every half hour to check for icebergs. On sunny days, she found time to read novels, knit a sweater, watch spectacular sunsets, and write in her logbook, where she kept an account of the weather and of her problems and pleasures. She started doing yoga. She chatted on her two-way radio with people who gave her weather reports, told her jokes, and cheered her on.

Most everyday routines took longer at sea. When it rained, she set buckets on the deck to collect water that ran off the mainsail. Unfortunately, waves splashed and sprayed into the bucket, making the rainwater almost as salty as the sea. Kay washed her clothes and sheets by soaking them in buckets of ocean water with detergent, then jumping up and down in the bucket to loosen stains. For the rinse cycle, she tied her shirts, shorts, and sheets to ropes and dragged them behind the boat. She wrung out her clothes and hung them on lines rigged beneath the sails. Once they were dry, she shook them to get out the salt, which made them crusty.

Kay spent most of Christmas Day coping with winds that hit sixty knots—sixty nautical miles per hour. She managed to reach her family, Ian, and a few friends on her two-way radio, opened the presents they had left, and heated up canned chicken, pumpkin, and potatoes.

During the following weeks, the temperature dipped to single digits. Kay wore all the thermal underwear and wool sweaters she could layer on. She grew anxious about passing Cape Horn, at the tip of South America. Winds and currents rushing down the continent's coasts often collided, creating massive storms. As Kay sailed nearer to shore, she kept a close eye on shipping lanes, where big tankers, freighters, and cargo carriers might pass by without picking up her sailboat on their radar screens. And while sailing near a coast put her closer to help if she needed it, she was also at greater risk of being spotted by drug smugglers or other criminals who might attempt to steal her sloop.

Kay sailed through cold, choppy water three miles from the shore of Cape Horn. She saw the high black cliffs that had dashed many tall ships, but the wind was kind that week. She called a cheery hello to some albatross soaring on the long, strong wings that carried them great distances. Kay headed north on the Atlantic Ocean, sailing about four thousand miles to the equator. Of course, she could get around the world more quickly by heading directly east to Africa, but in order to set an official maritime record for circumnavigation, she had to cross the equator as well as sail around the five southernmost capes.

At first, the weather grew even colder. Waves splashed on deck, spraying water that turned to ice. Kay gripped the safety lines as she crept across the deck to change sails or chip off ice, which made the rigging sag. Despite her caution, she slipped once. Her knee swelled, but she was grateful that no bones were broken. She never slept for more than twenty minutes at a time, but got up to check for ships, whales, or icebergs, which could destroy her boat. When she jotted notes in her logbook one evening, she was so tired that she forgot to keep moving her hand. The next day she found sentences scribbled over sentences, leaving a blur of words.

Fortunately, the air at last grew warmer as she traveled farther north. Kay stopped wearing jackets, then sweaters, then she took off her socks and shoes. Early in February, she rigged sheets over the deck to make a shady place. She poured buckets of water over herself to cool off. Now that she no longer had to watch for icebergs, she had time to fix a boom, the spar that holds the bottom of the mainsail, that had cracked in a storm. She changed the ropes so that they wouldn't wear out in the places where they were stressed. She oiled and tightened bolts and cables. She played solitaire. Every evening she felt cheered by sunsets that turned the sky yellow-gold or pink and red.

On February 25, she crossed the imaginary line of the equator. Now she was about halfway home. She opened a present her mother had wrapped for this occasion. Kay smiled as she dabbed her mother's favorite perfume on her wrists, bringing a sweet scent from home.

She headed south again, toward the tip of Africa, and coped with darker skies, rougher seas, and cold air. She felt the same anxiety she'd felt approaching the tip of South America. Kay thought Africa's Cape of Good Hope must have been named by someone who was awfully optimistic. Sailors called it the Cape of Storms.

A chilly fog hovered for seven days. Then thunder crashed. Lightning struck and exploded on the water. Hailstones clattered onto the deck. Kay took down the sails and retreated to the cabin, where she listened to the wind howl through the rigging. Her boat rocked wildly on enormous waves. She braced herself as the floor tilted up until, for several terrible moments, it became the wall.

After a few hours, the weather cleared enough for her to catch good winds and sail past Africa. She was happy to leave the Atlantic Ocean, but her pleasure didn't last long. Rain fell from clouds so thick that the sky turned pitch-black in the middle of the day. Waves as tall as the mast pushed her boat so that the bow pointed straight up. Her sailboat teetered on the wave's crest, then crashed back down. Another rogue wave tossed the boat briefly out of the sea, before slamming it back on the water. Kay stayed in the cabin, but crept up every twenty minutes, clipping on the safety harness, to check for damage and to scan the horizon for ships. Rain and splattering water stung her face.

Suddenly she saw lights slashing through the darkness. It didn't seem possible that anyone else would be out in a storm like this. But as the lights got brighter, Kay knew that a big ship was heading straight toward her. She blasted her horn and shouted into her microphone, "Turn! Turn!" She switched her two-way radio on to the emergency frequency, but waves and rain drowned out all other sounds. Kay raced around, turning on every light. While worrying that the freighter was coming too fast to stop even if someone saw her, she grabbed an emergency flare and ignited it. Wind blew the flare's flame and smoke toward a lashed sail. Thankfully, the wind changed and the flame dimmed. At least she hadn't burned down her boat.

But would she have to grab her identification papers and jump, trying her luck in the sea? Just as she began to lose hope, the massive freighter slowly turned just a little, but enough, to the side. Kay's boat bobbed in the water that churned in its wake. Her heart stopped pounding so hard.

Then a towering wave washed Kay off her boat, which tipped upside down.

She clung to the safety harness hitched to the boat. As waves shoved her deeper into the water, she hoped the ropes wouldn't snap. She held her breath and thought, *Come on, come on.* If one wave had been strong enough to knock over her boat, wouldn't another be able to turn it right side up?

She had almost run out of breath when a huge wave crashed, pushing her sloop back upright. Using almost her last bit of energy, Kay hauled herself up and over the railing.

Bruised and terrified, she bailed out water. She ducked under dripping sails and waded to the cabin. Cans of food, her half-finished knitting, tools, sneakers, and a teakettle sloshed across the flooded room. Kay fished out her teddy bear. She squeezed its soggy paws and touched her two-way radio. As soon as this storm let up, she could make a call and let someone know she was steering toward shore. She might even be able to catch a plane back to Australia. There were easier ways to get around the world than in a small boat.

But she thought, *If I can survive having my boat capsize in a storm, won't the coming days be easier?* She was alive, after all. *Blackmores First Lady* was battered, but not beyond repair.

The next morning, when the sky had cleared and the waves turned calmer, Kay knew she had a lot to be thankful for. She'd come this far by herself. Why shouldn't she make it the rest of the way home? She wrung out her clothes and picked up the rolling, clattering cans. She spread open her books on the deck to dry.

By the middle of April, Kay was about five thousand nautical miles from home. She crossed the Indian Ocean, where some days waves were high and fierce, since no landmasses were nearby to break their force. On other days, the winds blew gently. Large black and small brown dolphins played around her boat. Kay sat on the deck turning the damp pages of novels. She knit another sweater. As she approached Australia, she was happy to be near home, but anxious, too. Tides were strongest near shore. Hidden rocks or shoals could scrape and ruin the bottom of her boat.

She sailed south of her homeland. The sea was rough as she rounded the southernmost cape of Tasmania, but she kept the sloop steady. She had less than eight hundred miles to sail before reaching the city she'd left almost six months before. She was delighted to be back in the Pacific Ocean, where she was spared high winds and downpours, but light breezes made the going slow. She was sick of being patient. She was ready to take a bath in water that was not salty and to taste vegetables that didn't come from a can. She thought she'd never play solitaire again.

When Kay was close to Sydney, she radioed friends to let them know she was almost home. Then gales blew her sloop away from shore. With ten miles to go, she felt rain begin to fall. Kay picked up her two-way radio and was assured that everyone who'd come to greet her would wait until the sun came back out.

After a few hours, the rain stopped. Kay sailed closer to the white sand, the old lighthouse, fig trees, red-roofed houses, and Sydney's grand Opera House. Thousands of boats crowded the harbor. People climbed flagpoles on cruisers or waved from the crosstrees of yachts.

"Congratulations!" they called. "Way to go!"

After 189 days at sea, Kay became the first woman to complete a solo, nonstop, unassisted voyage around the world. She grinned and waved. She wept when she caught sight of her mother and father aboard their sailboat.

"We'll meet you onshore!" her mother called.

Kay sailed past yachts, Windsurfers, fishing boats, ferries, and little rubber boats. She pulled up to a wharf, and thanked thousands of strangers who wanted to hear her tales. Now she wished to be with those who'd believed in her every day of her voyage, the people who'd been here when she left and were back to celebrate her return.

She hugged her mother, father, sisters, and Fredo. She kissed Ian and hoped they could remain friends, though she knew now that she had the strength to leave him. She'd look for someone more like herself, someone who was ready to start a family.

Kay Cottee would sail again, many times, though she'd never go as far alone. She didn't need to now. She knew the sea as well as she knew land. She knew the sky by spending months beneath it. She would never forget the winds that had kept her company around the world.

—

After returning from the voyage that fulfilled her lifelong dream, Kay Cottee (1954–   ) married, had a child, and began working for a waterfront museum in Sydney, Australia, which displays Blackmores First Lady.

HOW CAN WE FIND SECRETS
UNDER STONE AND SEA?
SUE HENDRICKSON

S ue Hendrickson strapped on flippers and an oxygen
tank, then dived into waves that seemed as restless as
she was. She spent most of the day drifting close to
the ocean floor. Sue made her living by collecting
seashells and fish, which she sold to shops and aquariums.
After several years, her diving skills led to another job, finding and exploring ships that had sunk near Florida's coast.
Sue enjoyed working with the sky or sea overhead, but whenever she visited her parents back in Indiana, she heard how
worried her mother was about her sleeping on a sailboat tied
to a wharf. Sue wasn't earning much money: she didn't even
own a mirror, and just glanced at her reflection in the toaster
when combing her long blond hair. Sue's mom pointed out
that other girls her age lived in dormitories or apartments
and showed some interest in settling down.

Sue considered going to college, but after talking to some professors in the early 1970s, she realized that even with a college degree she'd wind up doing what she was doing now. Underwater salvage work seemed like a good job for a girl who'd been annoyed by people who told her to smile or speak up and never noticed that a shy person might see things that chatty people missed.

Sometimes Sue left Florida's southern coast to dive in the West Indies, where the green-blue sea lapped the pale sand. She admired the simple way that many people lived on these islands. She was twenty-five when some friends talked her into taking enough time away from the Dominican Republic beaches to climb one of the island's mountains. There Sue met miners who extracted amber, a clear yellow-brown stone often sold for jewelry. Amber had been formed from resin dripping from trees millions of years ago. The resin had hardened, sometimes trapping prehistoric insects, which became preserved in the midst of a crawl or flutter.

Sue took a break from her undersea work to search for chunks of amber with insects hidden between dark lines and speckles. She sold the best specimens of beetles, scorpions, plant hoppers, praying mantises, centipedes, and butterflies to natural history museums. She read books about insects and prehistory and asked experts lots of questions. Like self-educated Mary Anning, who became the first person to make a living by collecting fossils in the early nineteenth century, Sue Hendrickson didn't have a college degree, but she became highly respected by the scientists who studied the fossils she found.

"Don't you ever want to keep the amber?" some people

asked, admiring the stones, which were clear and yellow, like captured bits of sunlight.

"I just like finding things. I'm not a collector." Sue didn't like to own much more than she could carry in a knapsack. Even something beautiful would need to be packed or put away when she wanted to swim or wander to a new place, where she hoped to be astonished.

When Sue was offered a chance to look for bigger, even older fossils, she told her parents, "I'm going to Peru."

"South America!" her mother exclaimed. "Is it safe?"

"I'll get a dog," Sue said. "I'll be fine."

Sue traveled to a desert, where she joined a team hunting for fossils of whales, seals, and dolphins. She felt in a peculiar state of grace while chipping away stone to uncover traces of animals that had lived back when the desert had been sea. Stone fins and flippers were evidence of how the world had changed, so slowly that no one could witness its journey. Day after day, Sue aimed a chisel at rock, then swung her hammer. In rare moments, time seemed to slip aside and she glimpsed another world.

During the evenings, she talked around a campfire with people who shared her curiosity about ancient life. In 1986, one of these paleontologists, Peter Larson, invited Sue to work with him in South Dakota the following summer. Sue joined a small group working in the heat of the high plains. These people had dreams of finding a whole dinosaur skeleton, but they were content to excavate the backbones of duck-billed dinosaurs and triceratops horns. The finds weren't especially dramatic, but they were enough to keep Sue looking.

Near the end of her fourth summer in South Dakota, Sue

watched the three men on the excavating team climb into a truck. They were taking a couple of flat tires to town.

"Come on with us, Sue. We've been working hard for weeks," Peter Larson said. "While the tires get fixed, we can buy something cold to drink. We can eat a lunch that doesn't have sand in it. Sit in an air-conditioned place."

The temperature on August 12, 1990, was over one hundred degrees. Sue could think of more pleasant ways to spend the day than walking across the badlands, but for the past two weeks some distant cliffs had drawn her attention. Most of Sue's success as a collector came from looking patiently, but she also found things by following hunches. She wasn't mystical, but she'd learned to pay attention when she was drawn toward a place for no particular reason. Her hunches didn't always or even often pan out, but she respected them, if only because they wouldn't leave until she'd shrugged and looked.

"It sounds good, but I think I'll stay here," Sue said. She knew that people like Peter, who'd spent most of his life hunting for dinosaur bones in rocks, understood that a lot of things couldn't be explained. Still, she didn't want to be teased about a feeling that most likely would come to nothing. Sue waved goodbye to her friends and called her dog. "Let's go for a walk, Gypsy!"

She headed to the cliffs. For four hours, almost the only sounds she heard were her footsteps on dirt and rocks and the panting of her golden retriever.

When Sue reached the cliffs, she spotted a few old bones on the ground. She picked one up, then almost dropped it in surprise. Unlike the heavy bones of plant eaters like duckbills or triceratops, this fossil was light enough to make her think it was hollow. That meant the bones could be those of a carnivore.

Sue looked up to scan the cliffs. Three long backbones appeared faintly in the sandstone. Instead of the curved backbones she'd found before, these big vertebrae were straight. That was another sign of a carnivore. An enormous meat eater could mean these were the fossilized bones of a *Tyrannosaurus rex*. Could these bones have belonged to the huge, fierce dinosaur that had roamed here about sixty-seven million years ago? Sue reminded herself that only eleven incomplete *T. rex* skeletons had ever been found.

She hurried back to camp, where Peter Larson had returned from town. She said, "I think I've found something. Big."

"We're just finishing up for the season!"

"Come take a look," Sue insisted.

Peter took a second glance at Sue, grabbed her elbow, and said, "Which way?" They started running. Peter's mouth fell open as he gazed at the traces of the three backbones. They reached back into the cliff, which meant that the rest of the skeleton might be held there.

The next day, Sue, Peter, and their teammates lugged shovels, picks, and hammers to the site. They split open rock, spending thirteen-hour days in heat that rose to over 120 degrees Fahrenheit. By the end of three weeks, they'd cut out a huge block of stone. Inside it were the fossilized bones of a dinosaur that had been taller than many trees, and perhaps toppled some with a swing of her mighty tail. The stone would be shipped to a laboratory, where paleontologists would spend months chipping away sandstone with increasingly smaller chisels, carefully remove the fossilized bones, then fit them all together.

Even experts don't know enough about *T. rex* fossils to tell for certain the difference between male and female specimens, but the team members were aware that those bones had once been part of a living creature, and they wanted to give the dinosaur a name. They theorized that it had been female. "We'll name her Sue after you," Peter said. "It was an amazing find."

"I was lucky." Sue gazed at the broken cliffs, remembering the traces of three bones, pale as shadows. Sue's luck was the result of four summers she had spent swinging a hammer, the years she'd given up such luxuries as daily showers, a comfortable bed, and even little things such as lunch in an air-conditioned diner, chatting with friends and sipping an ice-cold drink instead of lukewarm tea from a thermos. She'd read hundreds of books, talked to dozens of scientists, and become an expert in the field.

Sue packed her duffel bag, called her dog, hugged her friends, and said goodbye.

"Where are you off to now?" Peter asked.

"Someplace where Gypsy and I can go for a swim."

Sue joined a team of marine archaeologists headed by Franck Goddio. They dived in the South China Sea to find a ship that had sunk four hundred years before. Swimming over smashed decks and between broken masts, Sue helped find antique cannon, blue-and-white plates decorated with birds and flowers, and pieces from a chess set that made her wonder about the last people who'd held the sculpted horses and small castles. Had a brother and sister plunked their elbows beside a checkered board? Had the chess game been played by tired sailors or a captain and his best friend?

The following year, Sue traveled with Franck Goddio's team to Egypt to look for one of Napoleon's warships. They found gold and silver coins, swords, and several shoes underwater. The team stayed in Egypt to explore Alexandria's harbor, where a fourth-century earthquake had toppled Cleopatra's summer palace into the sea. The divers salvaged bits of ancient blue glass and broken statues of pharaohs. In the murky green water, Sue often couldn't see her own hand when she stretched out her arm, so a sunken sphinx surprised her. Its human face had been worn away by waves. The lion-shaped body was encrusted with barnacles.

Sue found columns from temples dedicated to Poseidon, the Greek god of the sea, and Isis, the beloved Egyptian goddess. She swam over broken pavement, where Cleopatra might have walked while plotting battles and romances. Sue wondered if the Queen of the Nile ever got tired of pomp, power, and barges filled with rose petals. Did she ever long to find a stone where she could sit and listen to the sounds of the river?

After Sue's dog, Gypsy, died, she got another golden retriever, which she named Skywalker. She took him to Chicago, Illinois, in May 2000, when the dinosaur named Sue was unveiled in the grand hall at the center of the Field Museum of Natural History. Children and adults gasped at the forty-two-foot-long dinosaur, which was the biggest, most complete *Tyrannosaurus rex* yet found.

In recognition of her contributions to paleontology and

marine archaeology, Sue Hendrickson was awarded an honorary Ph.D. from the University of Illinois. For the occasion, she wore a traditional black gown and a flat tasseled cap over her blond hair, which she still kept long, only occasionally trimming it with her Swiss Army knife. She held up her diploma while her proud mother snapped pictures.

Sue continued spending most nights in tents, boats, or hotels, but a year before she'd turned fifty, in 1998, she had bought a house on an island in the West Indies. She and her dog, Skywalker, recipient of one and a half million airline miles, stayed there between excursions.

Sue waded into the blue-green sea and looked toward the distance, where the water's color deepened to the blue of the sky. Beyond places she could see were continents with long rivers, high mountains, wide deserts, fields of ice, and deep forests still to be explored. She picked up a smooth stone and tossed it into deep water.

"Let's go!" Sue called to her dog. They ran across the sand.

—

Sue Hendrickson (1949–) continues to explore land and sea. She dreams of traveling to the coldest regions of Russia to search the ice for the remains of a woolly mammoth. She says, "Being able to go wherever the next project takes me— and not knowing where that might be!—is as important to me as breathing."

HOW CAN WE REACH THE ENDS OF THE EARTH?
ANN BANCROFT

Standing on top of the tallest and coldest mountain in North America on June 18, 1983, Ann Bancroft took a picture of her climbing buddy. Others had been there before, but Ann felt proud. Summiting Mount McKinley had been a long-held dream of hers.

"Do you think we should turn around?" Ann asked.

Tim Elgren murmured words that got lost in the cold wind. Ann shrugged and took a few pictures of the snow-covered slopes and puffy clouds. It had taken Tim and her two weeks to climb the mountain's more than twenty thousand feet, stopping to pitch a tent each night. It had taken even longer to plan this trip from Minnesota to Alaska. Ann hated to turn around after ten minutes on the top, but the winds were fierce and cold, and it was a long way back to their tent.

"Ready to go?" she asked again.

Tim mumbled something she couldn't make out.

"Who are you talking to?" she asked.

"I don't know," he muttered. "They're your friends."

Ann took a closer look at Tim. His whole body seemed to shiver. She realized his blood must have turned so cold that he'd begun to hallucinate. At age twenty-eight, Ann had done enough winter camping and taught enough outdoor education to know her friend could die if he didn't warm up soon.

"Hey, it's okay," she said. She clipped one end of a safety rope to his belt and the other end to hers. This rope had kept them together as they'd climbed, so each could help the other if one slipped. Now both of their lives would depend on her strength and judgment.

I can't do this, Ann thought, then said, "Come on. We'll take this one step at a time."

Tim murmured and flapped his hands at people only he could see. Ann let him shiver, which she knew was the body's natural way of trying to warm up. As they started down, she slammed her ice ax with enough strength to hold them both to slippery and steep surfaces. They reached their tent at midnight.

The next day they continued down to slightly warmer regions. Tim started feeling better, and in another week they returned safely to the wide base of the mountain.

Soon Ann was back at her job in Minnesota, teaching gym in an elementary school. She kept in touch with Tim, who was doing fine. One day he said that Will Steger, a science teacher turned expedition leader, wanted her to visit his camp in the woods of northern Minnesota. Tim didn't say what Will wanted, but Ann decided to go up for a weekend. She'd heard the area was a great place to cross-country ski.

After Ann checked out some trails and Will showed her the huskies he was training as sled dogs, he said, "Tim told me you saved his life up on Denali." Will used the old Athabascan Indian name for Mount McKinley, which meant "the Great One."

"We were a team," Ann shrugged. "If I'd come down with hypothermia, he would have done the same for me."

"You stayed calm when others might have panicked," Will said. "Tim says you have lots of experience with winter camping."

"I was eight when I started talking my cousins into camping in the woods behind our house." Ann watched the gray-and-white puppies wag their curly tails and bound onto each other.

"You must get along with people pretty well if you could convince kids to sleep out in the snow."

"Some cousins ran back to my family's farmhouse after ten minutes, but I was lucky. I have a lot of cousins and four brothers and sisters. I guess we had to figure out how to get along." Ann looked at Will. Surely he hadn't asked her there to talk about her childhood.

"Tim says you teach phys ed," Will said.

"It gets me outdoors about half the year, anyway," Ann said. She didn't want to sound corny, so she didn't add that she liked encouraging students who had a better chance of doing well on fields or basketball courts than they did with a piece of paper. The sort of kid she had been.

"I'm putting together a team to trek to the North Pole," Will said. "Would you be interested?"

Stunned by the change of subject, Ann could almost hear the sound of a book sliding off her father's shelves. She remembered opening it to pictures of a broken ship sinking between blocks of ice. She'd been twelve, and had just taken tests that showed she had dyslexia. Having a name for her learning disability didn't stop words and numbers from bobbing or knotting like fists, instead of settling into sensible patterns. Much more helpful was finding a book on her father's shelf, the first book that seemed worth the effort of unscrambling sentences. Lured by pictures of a beautiful old ship sinking between blocks of ice, Ann read about Ernest Shackleton's 1914 dream of crossing Antarctica. This changed to a dream of survival when he and twenty-eight men watched their ship, the *Endurance*, sink. Ann read about how every one of those polar explorers made it home. A dream took shape in her own mind.

"We'll cross five hundred miles of ice, maybe more," Will said. "I expect the Arctic trip to take two months."

"Count me in," Ann said.

Ann and the other adventurers built sleds to carry their equipment. They trained and practiced with huskies and other sled dogs. The trip was to be much like the one Robert Peary had made about seventy-five years before. Instead of taking a ship, they would fly to the northernmost edge of land, but then, like the explorers of old, they'd rely on dogs to help pull the sleds. They would take radios, but use them only if someone's health or life was in danger.

Their trip would not be resupplied, which meant they had

to pack whatever they might need. Since the explorers and dogs would be hauling everything on sleds, they didn't want extra weight. They planned to wear one outfit and get used to being smelly. They cut toothbrushes in half. Figuring she'd need three ounces of toothpaste for two months, Ann squeezed all but that from a tube.

In March 1986, Ann, seven men, and forty-nine dogs flew on a small cargo plane to the northernmost point of North America. Ann Bancroft, Will Steger, Paul Schurke, Robert McKerrow, Brent Boddy, Geoff Carroll, Bob Mantell, and Richard Weber unloaded sleds and supplies. Working quickly in the cold fog, they set up two tents along the shore. They made supper and crawled fully dressed into their sleeping bags.

The next morning, one of the three men who shared a tent with Ann crawled back in and reported, "The liquid in our thermometer turned solid. The temperature must have dropped below minus sixty degrees Fahrenheit." It took an hour to melt enough snow to make oatmeal.

Ann melted a dab of her frozen toothpaste over the small gas stove. Of course, there were no bathrooms, so she walked a short way from the tent, swiftly unzipped her pants, and crouched on the snow. This made her thighs more vulnerable to frostbite than the men's, but otherwise being the only woman on the team didn't make much difference. It was a bigger problem being the shortest member, which meant she'd have to work harder to cover the same amount of ground.

The sun shone for twenty minutes the first day; but with spring coming, it would stay out longer every day. Tides had pushed water that had frozen, melted, split, and piled, over thousands of years, into hills of broken ice. The explorers spent about ten hours pushing sleds loaded with food, fuel, and equipment over these pressure ridges, or slabs of broken ice, and covered only one and a half miles that first day. They had about 499 miles to go.

Ann and the seven men hoped the ice and snow would be smoother as they got away from land. Sometimes it was, but shifting currents below the ice often broke it and left mounds that were higher than houses and miles long. The explorers looked for gaps in the ice ridges, chopped out a pathway, or let the dogs rest while they pulled and shoved their sleds over the jumbled blocks. When it was Ann's turn to stay with the dogs, she stamped her feet and swung her arms to coax her warm blood toward her fingers and toes.

Near the end of their first week in the Arctic, a sled Robert McKerrow was pushing tipped over on him. Despite badly bruised ribs that might be broken, he kept on. So did Bob Mantell, though after ten days of cold the tips of four of his toes were black with frostbite. Ann's face felt as stiff as wood. Her friends' noses were black or peeling from frostbite. Their skin was swollen and scabbed, and everyone had sore muscles. But there was no use in crying in a place so cold that tears froze eyelids shut. Besides, Ann felt strangely at home in the stark white landscape.

They rested only during blizzards, when the snow blew so thickly that they could barely see. Robert's chest ached so much that he had a hard time breathing, and there were lots of bad colds going around.

Every night the explorers pounded their sleeping bags to break up ice, which had formed when the moisture from their bodies collected and froze. Paul took readings with a sextant, measuring the angle between where they stood and the sun or stars, to determine their location.

At the end of the third week, Robert said, "I can't go on."

Everyone nodded. Ann was disappointed for him, but she understood that he had no other choice. Will radioed for a plane to fly Robert home. Some dogs were also airlifted out: fewer were needed now because the sleds were lighter, since they'd used up food and fuel. And a few sleeping bags that had become so caked with ice that they weighed fifty pounds were sent back, too. From then on, the explorers zipped together two sleeping bags for three people to share each night, while the seventh person kept his own sleeping bag. As the shortest person in her tent, Ann was chosen for the middle. Sleeping between two friends was crowded, but it helped Ann warm up more quickly. Before slipping into the sleeping bag, Ann sometimes used half a mug of melted ice to take a quick "bath."

On the following days, the temperature rose to thirty or forty degrees below zero. The air felt more comfortable, but the ice beneath the explorers' feet was in more danger of breaking up. Ann was alert to cracking sounds, and prepared to run if the ice beneath her split open. More and more often the explorers faced gaps of water between the big plates of ice they walked on. If these leads, or open strips of water, weren't too wide, everyone jumped over them. If the ice near the water was thin, they followed the leads to find a place where the ice on either side came together. Sometimes they set up their tents and waited for the colder night air to freeze the sea's surface by morning.

One day during their fifth week out, Ann turned her back

to the Arctic water to coax the dogs to jump across a lead. The ice beneath her shattered. Her feet plunged into the water. She flung out her arms and gripped the edge of the ice before she sank more than waist-deep in the sea. She climbed out, while Paul tore through a sled to find spare pants and socks. Ann changed clothes in record time. She shivered for the next two days.

Ann knew that if the weather held, they might reach their goal in another week or two. But anything could happen on what was probably the most dangerous part of the trip. Bob Mantell's frostbitten feet became increasingly painful as they crossed miles of rough, ragged ice. Will called on the two-way radio for a small plane to take Bob home.

Ann and the five remaining men silently watched the plane fly away. She would miss her friend, as she missed Robert, and she grieved for their bad luck and lost chances. Though Ann sometimes daydreamed about warm kitchens, she kept going not only for herself but for anyone who might be waiting to see if she would become the first woman to reach the North Pole on foot.

The six remaining explorers continued heading north. They reached a crack in the ice and followed the lead to a spot where it narrowed to a width of eight feet. Each of the five men took a running start and jumped across the black water. The dogs swam to the other side, shook themselves, and sped around the ice to warm up. Ann stared into the water, wishing she weren't the shortest person on the team. Legs even an inch or two longer could mean the difference between landing safely or tumbling into the two-mile-deep sea.

"You can do it, Ann!" Will, Paul, Brent, Geoff, and Richard called.

Ann ran, leaped, and stretched her legs as far as they would go. One foot landed on solid ice. Her other foot followed. She swung up her arms and whooped.

For two more weeks, Ann and the men pushed sleds, jumped over cracks in the ice, and pitched tents, which were frosted each morning from their moist breath. On May 1, 1986, they reached the North Pole. The ice and sky didn't look much different from anything they'd seen during most of the previous two months, but they had done what they'd set out to do. Ann had changed from someone who wondered if she could reach the North Pole to someone who knew that she had done so.

A plane carrying reporters flew to meet the team and take pictures. Then they all crowded into an airplane, where someone handed Ann an apple. After weeks of eating warm, mushy food, it was good to hear her teeth crunch through the fruit's red skin, to taste something fresh and sweet. But Ann kept looking back, hoping to see the curving edge of the earth. She was already forgetting how her fingers had ached and her skin stung in the cold.

At home in Minnesota, she was happy to take a shower, wash her hair, smell pine trees, see her family, and climb into a warm bed. But the thought of spending the rest of her life driving between work, home, and a grocery store made her feel as if she might as well spin in a small circle. Why should her adventures be over? After all, the world had more than one Pole.

Ann looked for other women who shared her dream of

crossing Antarctica. She met Sue Giller, Sunniva Sorby, and Anne Dal Vera, all experienced mountain climbers and skiers. The four women began training and looking for sponsors to help buy equipment and cover the enormous expense of traveling to and from Antarctica. Ann approached more than 250 government or business organizations, but the only company that offered support sold cigarettes, and the women declined.

The women, who named their team AWE, abbreviated from American Women's Trans-Antarctic Expedition, turned to schools. Teachers, kids, and moms realized that the trip across the coldest, windiest continent on Earth was dangerous, but they believed it was possible and important. They organized bake sales, car washes, penny collections, and can drives. They sent checks that were usually small and notes that were always enthusiastic.

Ann borrowed the rest of the money they needed. After five years of planning and practicing with skis and sleds, the AWE team flew to the Hercules Inlet on Antarctica's shore. With numb fingers, they struggled to set up two tents in sixty-mile-per-hour winds. They built snow walls to help break the wind, organized their equipment, and tried to sleep. On November 9, 1992, they strapped on skis and set out across pale pink, blue, and white snow.

Almost every morning they got up at six o'clock. They took turns melting snow to make hot chocolate and oatmeal with dried cherries. Everyone put on sunscreen, sunglasses, and layers of warm clothes. They rolled up the tents, piled everything onto four sleds, which they pulled by themselves, checked the compass, and headed south. They skied about ten hours a day, often over bumpy terrain and uphill into fierce winds. They usually skied in a line, taking turns at being the leader. It was harder work to break tracks, but the person who skied in front had the finest view.

After weeks of crossing hundreds of miles of snow, everyone had sore muscles. The sleds felt heavier, though they were actually lighter, since some of the food had been eaten. Sunniva Sorby became ill with bronchitis and sprained her ankle. Then Anne Dal Vera hurt her legs. They had been skiing every day for six weeks when she said, "I don't think I can go on."

"You can. We've got to." Ann offered aspirin, bandages, and encouraging words, but she couldn't give her friends time to rest, which was what she knew they needed for their injuries to heal.

On January 1, Sunniva said she would struggle to get to the South Pole but that she wanted to leave from there rather than continue across Antarctica.

A few days later, Anne Dal Vera said she'd leave at the South Pole, too.

Ann Bancroft nodded, trying to understand.

"We can't keep going, but there are still two of you who can," Sunniva told Ann. "Will you and Sue cross the continent?"

"For now, let's just focus on making sure all of us get to the South Pole," Ann said. Each woman had to make her own decision about how much cold and pain she could bear, but as leader, Ann had to decide when to end the trip.

She tucked her chin and skied into wind that charged toward them like an opposing army. Hour after hour, she heard the scraping, squeaking, and shush of skis on snow. They had skied for more than two months and covered almost seven hundred miles, when Ann saw the domed top of the South Pole research station.

On January 14, 1993, scientists and staff wearing red parkas ran out to greet them. "Congratulations!" a few dozen people cried. "Way to go!"

Ann, Sue, Sunniva, and Anne skied past the flags of the countries that peacefully shared the continent. They touched their gloved hands, all at once, to the red-and-white-striped pole. They grinned at their reflections in the silver ball on its top.

"Let's get a picture of the first woman to trek to the North Pole and the South Pole, too!" People aimed their cameras at Ann. She smiled, but when they invited her into the research station to celebrate with a cup of hot coffee, she shook her head. She craved silence and snow more than praise or parties. And she had to decide whether she and Sue should go home from here or continue the journey.

Ann skied across the white fields, which demanded strength and courage, but never more than she had to give. They made her heart feel wide. How could she stop, she wondered, when she still had the will to go on? Would the teachers, moms, and kids who'd helped the team get here feel let down that the trip had been cut short? Or would they be relieved that the members had returned safely? Ann knew that a second plane would cost more than thirty thousand dollars, and they were already in debt.

This team came here together, Ann thought. *We should leave together, too.*

As the four women flew home from Antarctica, Ann

couldn't help feeling that she'd achieved just half of a dream. She cheerfully greeted friends and family in Minnesota, then began earning money to repay the team's debts by traveling around the country, speaking about the trip.

Ann Bancroft never stopped wondering what she would do next. A year after the AWE expedition, she heard that a Norwegian woman named Liv Arnesen had just become the first woman to ski alone to the South Pole. Ann arranged to meet her in 1998. Like Ann, Liv was in her forties and had been a teacher. She was an expert skier, was married and had a grown daughter, and had climbed on a Mount Everest expedition.

"What got you interested in Antarctica?" Ann asked.

"It might sound crazy, but ever since I was twelve, I was never able to get the frozen continent out of my mind. I read a book about how Ernest Shackleton and his team survived after their ship, the *Endurance*, sank in the ice."

"It doesn't sound crazy." Ann smiled, remembering the pictures of the doomed ship in the book she'd found on her father's shelf. "Do you think a team of two would be the right size to make it all the way across Antarctica?"

"Why not?" Liv said.

Perhaps since both women had already shown they could ski to the South Pole, they were quite successful in raising funds. A car company paid for some equipment, and the U.S. Army loaned satellite phones. Ann and Liv could use these to call for help in an emergency and to communicate with the thousands of students who would follow the course of their trip via computers in the classroom. After two years of planning and training, which included lots of mountain climbing and holding sails aloft while crossing beaches, Ann and Liv flew to Queen Maud Land in Antarctica.

Starting on November 14, 2000, they spent twelve-hour days dragging sleds that weighed about 250 pounds. They cross-country skied up the Sygyn Glacier until they reached ice that was split open in many places. They strapped crampons on their boots and edged their way past crevasses that might be thousands of feet deep.

Each night they looked for a safe place to set up their tent. They used a GPS, a global navigation system, to determine their location and wrote their latitude, longitude, and altitude on the inside roof of their red tent. Since the sun was out all night during Antarctica's summer season, before they went to sleep they set out solar panels that recharged the batteries of their satellite phones.

When they reached fairly flat snow-covered land, they held aloft sails while they skied. The sails were four different sizes and shapes and were chosen according to the wind's force, with the biggest used to catch the lightest breezes. As wind filled the sails, Ann and Liv glided over smooth snow but bumped and clattered over wind-sculpted snow, which had frozen in the shape of ocean waves. They sped to the peaks, sailed briefly with air beneath their skis, clattered down, then bounded over another wave of frozen snow, and another.

This was sometimes fun, but it wasn't easy to keep the more than a dozen lines attached to the sails from tangling while dragging sleds behind them. Ann and Liv had to make sure they didn't pick up too much speed and sail into ice towers or over holes. High winds threatened to tip them over. After about fifteen minutes, their arms and shoulders ached from holding the billowing sails aloft. Their arms hurt even more after an hour, and at the end of a ten- or twelve-hour day the last thing the women wanted to do was raise their arms again.

But that's what they did the next morning. They rested only on days when blowing snow made the air as white as the ground. Then they stayed in their tent and mended sails. When they ran out of thread, they used dental floss, which made the sails smell faintly of mint.

On January 16, 2001, after covering about thirteen hundred miles in sixty-four days, Ann and Liv reached the striped pole topped with the silver ball. They enjoyed a cup of coffee in the South Pole research station, chatted with scientists, took a shower, and put on clean clothes. But, sleeping in their tent that night, they were annoyed by the racket from the station's generators. The South Pole wasn't exactly a city, but after days of seeing only each other on the ice, it seemed noisy and crowded. Ann and Liv left the following day.

They spent a week skiing up the slopes of Titan Dome, then made their slow, careful way past crevasses on the long glacier that runs through the Transantarctic Mountains. Beyond these mountains was the ice-covered sea, the other side of the continent. Some ridges were so steep that Ann and Liv tied their sleds together. Ann pulled the sleds in front, while Liv held the backs to keep the sleds from dashing down too quickly and crashing into Ann. When the women reached bare rock, they carried their skis and sleds.

By February 2001, they'd spent ninety-four days skiing, hiking, and sailing more than seventeen hundred miles. They'd reached the continent's other side. Ann was cold. She was tired. Almost every muscle in her body ached. She was as happy as she'd ever been.

Ann used the satellite phone to call for an airplane to pick them up on the Ross Ice Shelf. She gave their precise location, but since the sun hadn't been out for a week, the solar batteries on their phone were low. She heard more crackling than words. She hoped the pilots could hear better and that the wind would die down. The sky needed to be clear enough of clouds and blowing snow for a pilot to navigate through air in which it was hard to tell the ice from the white sky.

They waited a day before Ann got word that a plane was on the way. She and Liv lined up their sleeping bags, knapsacks, skis, and red tent to mark a runway on the snow that covered the ice.

Finally they heard the racket of an engine and propellers.

"Stop!" Ann and Liv shouted, though they knew their voices couldn't reach the pilots. "Here we are!" Two women on a huge expanse of snow.

The plane turned around and navigated through the white sky to the snow-covered ice. As the Twin Otter plane landed, its skis scraped away snow to expose two deep crevasses. The plane pulled past the split ice, then the pilot and the co-pilot jumped out.

"You made it!" Ann said.

"Yes, barely. We're not going back up there today. We can't see much and only caught sight of your red tent after we'd turned around."

The pilots set up a tent near Ann and Liv's. They waited another day. During the middle of the second night, the wind died down, and one pilot said, "Let's go for it!"

Everyone packed in a hurry, before the weather changed

again. As Ann dashed for the plane, the surface beneath her feet gave way. She flung out her arms to catch herself as she fell waist-deep into a crevasse.

"Let's get out of here!" the pilot shouted.

Ann hauled herself out of the crevasse. She and Liv jumped into the plane. As it rose, they looked down at the broken ice, the dangerous, beautiful world.

Snow had already covered their tracks, but Ann knew the width of a frozen continent with every muscle of her body. The journey had changed not only her but the world. The hope raised by two strong women's determination would never disappear.

—

Ann Bancroft (1955–   ) and Liv Arnesen (1953–   ) have continued to make long journeys over land.

Ann Bancroft has traveled to almost every state in the United States and to several countries. She and Liv Arnesen talk about their trips and plan new ones. They encourage others to learn about the world outside their windows and to let dreams lead them around that world.

Since the 1993 AWE Expedition, all the team members have been back to Antarctica. Sue Giller (1946–   ) returned to help field scientists. Anne Dal Vera (1953–   ) spent time working in U.S. bases. Sunniva Sorby (1960–   ) often lectures aboard icebreakers in the Arctic and Antarctica.

There have always been girls who looked at the sea, stars, prairies, and forests and wondered what lay beyond what they could see. Some grew up to cross deserts on camels or ice on skis, to climb up mountains or crawl into caves, to sail over or swim under the sea. From the hundreds who have made history, I chose to focus on twelve women from around the globe whose lives show the progress in about 240 years of exploring the coldest and the hottest, the highest and the deepest regions of land and sea.

I read books, diaries, and letters, then imagined sounds and sights suggested by these accounts of true adventures and accomplishments. As a portrait painter might change colors or shapes to reveal deeper truths about a real person, I created dialogue to fashion summaries into scenes.

I tried to keep these episodes within a framework of known facts, and the major events can be verified. When faced with vague or contradictory information, I relied on what was certain to make my best guess at the truth. Stories change through time and translation. People's memories are unique and imperfect, and most explorers are more focused on survival than on record-keeping. Since written language is fairly recent in parts of Africa, the Amazon, and the Arctic, standardized spelling of names and places couldn't always be found, in which case I generally chose the spelling used by the explorers.

It was a pleasure and a privilege to write about these trailblazers. Many had formed dreams of faraway places when they were not much younger or older than eleven. Some had mothers who waved goodbye when their brave, restless, and curious daughters set out for dangerous places, and who welcomed them home with joy.

These girls grew into women who were fascinated by maps, the outdoors, seeing and doing what no woman had seen and done before. They defined themselves not only by where they'd come from but also by where they dared to go. Sometimes they were lonely and afraid, but each found brave spaces in her heart. None ever gave up. They believed that every journey begins with questions—and a dream.

IMPORTANT YEARS IN WOMEN'S EXPLORATION HISTORY

1766: JEANNE BARET disguises herself as a boy and leaves France to become the first woman to sail around the world.

1864: FLORENCE BAKER and her husband, Samuel Baker, travel about half the length of Africa. They discover one of the main sources of the Nile River to be Lake Albert.

1869: The Dutch explorer ALEXANDRINE TINNÉ becomes the first European woman to attempt to cross the Sahara Desert, where she is murdered. Her name is engraved on a stone monument in southern Sudan, along with those of Florence and Samuel Baker and other Nile River explorers.

1891: JOSEPHINE DIEBITSCH PEARY becomes the first non-native woman to cross the Arctic Circle in Greenland when she joins her husband, Robert Peary, on five expeditions before his 1909 claim to have reached the North Pole.

1908: At age fifty-eight, ANNIE SMITH PECK summits Mount Huascarán, the highest mountain in Peru. She is honored as the first woman to summit a mountain no person has yet climbed.

1921: ARNARULUNGUAQ, an Inuit woman, joins the Danish explorer Knud Rasmussen on a three-year journey across the top of North America, sailing, hiking, and driving a dogsled from Greenland to Alaska.

1926: ELISABETH CASTERET and her husband discover and explore the highest ice cave then on record, the Grotte Casteret. Elisabeth Casteret makes more than three hundred caving expeditions in Spain, Morocco, and her native France, a country that boasts some of the deepest caves in the world.

1952: NICOLE MAXWELL accidentally hurts herself with a machete while hiking in the Amazon, then devotes the rest of her life to studying healing plants from South American rain forests.

1955: DR. EUGENIE CLARK founds and becomes director of Cape Haze Marine Laboratory in Florida, where she oversees shark studies that take her to more than twenty-five countries and oceans around the world.

1975: JUNKO TABEI of Japan becomes the first woman to summit Mount Everest. She says, "Technique and ability alone do not get one to the top; it is the willpower that is most important. This willpower you cannot buy with money or be given by others. It rises from your heart."

1979: DR. SYLVIA EARLE sets a record for untethered diving when she plunges 1,250 feet undersea.

1984: KATY PAYNE, an acoustic biologist, spends a week carefully observing elephants in a Portland, Oregon, zoo and discovers that elephants communicate with each other via sounds humans can't hear. She spends much of the next twenty years researching and measuring infrasound to understand and protect elephants in Africa and India.

1986: ANN BANCROFT becomes the first woman to cross the ice to reach the North Pole.

1988: Although KRYSTYNA CHOJNOWSKA-LISKIEWICZ of Poland

is the first woman to sail solo around the world, in 1976–78, and TANIA AEBI is the first American woman and youngest person to sail around the world, in 1987, both women stopped at shores along the way. In 1988, KAY COTTEE of Australia becomes the first woman to complete a solo, nonstop voyage around the world.

1990: SUE HENDRICKSON discovers the largest, most complete *T. rex* skeleton yet found. She continues more than thirty years of expeditions, including work in Egypt, where in 2001 she helps to excavate Herakleion, the city of Hercules, which sank underwater in an earthquake that took place more than two thousand years ago.

1993: ANN BANCROFT and the American Women's Trans-Antarctic Expedition—a team that includes SUE GILLER, who has climbed major mountains in the Himalayas, South America, and Alaska, and ANNE DAL VERA and SUNNIVA SORBY, who are highly experienced skiers—become the first group of women to ski from the coast of Antarctica to the South Pole.

2001: ANN BANCROFT and the Norwegian LIV ARNESEN become the first women to cross Antarctica on foot, showing the power of dreams and determination.

SELECTED BOOKS AND WEB SITES

(Books noted with * were published for young readers.)

OVERVIEWS OF EXPLORERS

Polk, Milbry, and Mary Tiegreen. *Women of Discovery: A Celebration of Intrepid Women Who Explored the World*. New York: Clarkson Potter, 2001. This book features accounts of Jeanne Baret, Sylvia Earle, Sue Hendrickson, and about eighty other explorers, along with many stunning photographs.

Robinson, Jane. *Wayward Women: A Guide to Women Travellers*. Oxford: Oxford University Press, 1990.

Slung, Michele. *Living with Cannibals and Other Women's Adventures*. Washington, D.C.: National Geographic Society, 2000. This book includes chapters about Florence Baker, Sylvia Earle, and fourteen other adventurers not profiled here.

National Geographic Society: *http://www.nationalgeographic.org*. This Web site offers current news about science and discovery, including audio and video interviews with explorers. There are maps to download and special sections for students and teachers.

HOW WIDE IS THE WORLD? JEANNE BARET

Ross, Michael. *Bougainville*. London: Gordon and Cremonesi, 1978.

Stuart, David. *The Plants That Shaped Our Gardens*. Cambridge, Mass.: Harvard University Press, 2002.

HOW FAR CAN A RIVER FLOW? FLORENCE BAKER

Baker, Anne. *Morning Star: Florence Baker's Diary of the Expedition to Put Down the Slave Trade on the Nile, 1870–1873*. London: Kimber, 1972.

Baker, Samuel White. *The Albert N'yanza*. Vols. 1 and 2. New York: Horizon Press, 1962.

Hall, Richard. *Lovers on the Nile*. New York: Random House, 1980.

*McLoone, Margo. *Women Explorers in Africa*. Mankato, Minn.: Capstone Press, 1997.

Oliver, Caroline. *Western Women in Colonial Africa*. Westport, Conn.: Greenwood Press, 1982.

HOW CAN WE CLIMB WHERE NO ONE HAS GONE BEFORE? ANNIE SMITH PECK

Brown, Rebecca A. *Women on High*. Boston: Appalachian Mountain Club Books, 2002.

Olds, Elizabeth Fagg. *Women of the Four Winds*. Boston: Houghton Mifflin, 1985.

Peck, Annie Smith. *A Search for the Apex of America*. New York: Dodd, Mead, 1911.

HOW FAR NORTH CAN WE GO? JOSEPHINE PEARY

Astrup, Eivind. *With Peary Near the Pole*. Translated by H. J. Bull. London: C. Arthur Pearson Limited, 1898.

Bryce, Robert M. *Cook and Peary: The Polar Controversy, Resolved.* Mechanicsburg, Pa.: Stackpole Books, 1997.

Peary, Josephine Diebitsch. *My Arctic Journal: A Year Among Ice-Fields and Eskimos.* New York: Cooper Square Press, 2002.

———. *The Snow Baby.* New York: Frederick A. Stokes, 1901.

*Peary, Josephine Diebitsch, and Marie Peary. *Children of the Arctic.* Honolulu: University Press of the Pacific, 2001.

HOW CAN A CONTINENT BE CROSSED?
ARNARULUNGUAQ

Ehrlich, Gretel. *This Cold Heaven: Seven Seasons in Greenland.* New York: Pantheon Books, 2001.

Freuchen, Peter. *I Sailed with Rasmussen.* New York: Julian Messner, 1958.

Rasmussen, Knud. *Across Arctic America: Narrative of the Fifth Thule Expedition.* Fairbanks: University of Alaska Press, 1999.

HOW DEEP IS THE EARTH? ELISABETH CASTERET

*Aulenbach, Nancy Holler, and Hazel A. Barton, with Marfé Ferguson Delano. *Exploring Caves: Journeys into the Earth.* Washington, D.C.: National Geographic Society, 2001.

Casteret, Norbert. *The Darkness Under the Earth.* London: Dent, 1954.

———. "Discovering the Oldest Statues in the World." *National Geographic,* Aug. 1924.

———. *More Years Under the Earth.* Translated by Rosemary Dinnage. London: Scientific Book Club, 1962.

———. "Probing Ice Caves of the Pyrenees." *National Geographic,* March 1953.

———. *Ten Years Under the Earth.* Translated by Barrows Mussey. London: Dent, 1963.

HOW MANY SECRETS CAN BE FOUND IN A FOREST? NICOLE MAXWELL

Maxwell, Nicole. *Witch Doctor's Apprentice.* New York: Citadel Press, 1990.

HOW DEEP CAN WE DIVE? SYLVIA EARLE

*Butts, Ellen R., and Joyce R. Schwartz. *Eugenie Clark: Adventures of a Shark Scientist.* North Haven, Conn.: Linnet Books, 2000.

Clark, Eugenie. *The Lady and the Sharks.* Sarasota, Fla.: Mote Marine Laboratory, 1995.

*Earle, Sylvia A. *Dive! My Adventures in the Deep Frontier.* Washington, D.C.: National Geographic Society, 1999.

————. *Sea Change: A Message of the Oceans.* New York: Ballantine, 1995.

*McGovern, Ann. *Shark Lady: True Adventures of Eugenie Clark.* New York: Scholastic, 1978.

*McLoone, Margo. *Women Explorers of the Oceans.* Mankato, Minn.: Capstone Press, 2000.

Sylvia A. Earle: *http://literati.net/Earle/*

HOW HIGH CAN WE CLIMB? JUNKO TABEI

*McLoone, Margo. *Women Explorers of the Mountains.* Mankato, Minn.: Capstone Press, 2000.

Junko Tabei Interview:
http://www.nesaj.org/nesajpatra/march2002/tabeieng.htm

HOW FAR CAN WE SAIL ALONE? KAY COTTEE

Cottee, Kay. *First Lady.* Sydney: Pan Books, 1990.

HOW CAN WE FIND SECRETS UNDER STONE AND SEA?
SUE HENDRICKSON

Fiffer, Steve. *Tyrannosaurus Sue: The Extraordinary Saga of the Largest, Most Fought Over T. Rex Ever Found*. New York: W. H. Freeman, 2000.

*Hendrickson, Sue, as told to Kimberly Weinberger. *Hunt for the Past: My Life as an Explorer*. New York: Scholastic, 2001.

*Reif, Pat, with the SUE Science Team of The Field Museum. *A Dinosaur Named SUE: The Story of the Colossal Fossil, The World's Most Complete T. rex*. New York: Scholastic, 2000.

HOW CAN WE REACH THE ENDS OF THE EARTH?
ANN BANCROFT

Bancroft, Ann, and Liv Arnesen, with Cheryl Dahle. *No Horizon Is So Far: Two Women and Their Extraordinary Journey Across Antarctica*. Cambridge, Mass., and New York: Da Capo Press, 2003.

*Loewen, Nancy, and Ann Bancroft. *Four to the Pole! The American Women's Expedition to Antarctica, 1992–93*. North Haven, Conn.: Linnet Books, 2001.

Rothblum, Esther, Jacqueline S. Weinstock, and Jessica F. Morris, eds. *Women in the Antarctic*. Binghamton, N.Y.: Haworth Press, 1998.

Steger, Will, with Paul Schurke. *North to the Pole*. New York: Times Books, 1987.

Sullivan, Robert, and Robert Andreas. *The Greatest Adventures of All Time*. Des Moines: Life Books, 2000.

*Wenzel, Dorothy. *Ann Bancroft: On Top of the World*. Minneapolis: Dillon Press, 1990.

Adventures of Ann Bancroft and Liv Arnesen:
http://www.yourexpedition.com

INDEX

Aebi, Tania, 199
Ahnighito (Inuit woman), 61, 62, 65
Alaska, Arnarulunguaq in, 89–94
Albert, Lake, 36–38, 40, 41
Aleqasina (Inuit woman), 72
Amazon region, 50, 114–22, 198
American Women's Trans-Antarctic
    Expedition (AWE), 186–88, 190,
    194, 199
Andes range, 45–49, 50, 51–54, 55
Anning, Mary, 169
Antarctica
    American Women's Trans-Antarctic
        Expedition, 186–90, 194
    Bancroft and Arneson cross, 190–94
    Shackleton in, 180, 190
Arctic, *see under* Arnarulunguaq (Inuit
    woman); Bancroft, Ann; Peary,
    Josephine Diebitsch
Arnarulunguaq (Inuit woman), 77–96,
    198
    in Alaska, 90–94
    childhood, 78
    crosses Arctic Canada, 83–90
    death of husband, 82
    meets king of Denmark, 94–95
    personal relationship with Ras-
        mussen, 86–87, 89, 90–91
    son of, 89, 90, 92–94
    in United States, 90–94
    volunteers to go on Rasmussen expe-
        dition, 79–80
Arnesen, Liv, 190–94, 199
AWE (American Women's Trans-
    Antarctic Expedition), 186–88, 190,
    194, 199

Bacita (translator), 33, 35, 37, 38, 39
Baker, Florence von Sass, 24–41, 197
    auctioned as slave, 24, 25
    childhood, 24–25
    in England, 39–41
    meets and marries Samuel Baker, 25–
        27
    reaches a Nile River source, 36–38
    and search for Nile River source, 27–
        39
    on second Nile expedition, 41
Baker, Samuel
    discovers Murchison Falls, 39
    knighthood and honors, 40–41
    meets and marries Florence von Sass,
        25–27
    reaches a Nile River source, 36–38
    returns to England, 39–41
    searches for Nile River source, 26–39
    second Nile expedition, 41
Bancroft, Ann, 177–94, 199
    achievements of, 188, 194, 199
    ambition to cross Antarctica, 186
    crosses Antarctica, 190–94, 199
    first woman to reach both poles on
        foot, 188
    first woman to reach North Pole on
        foot, 185, 198
    and North Pole expedition, 180–85,
        198
    South Pole trek with AWE, 186–88,
        199
    summits Mount McKinley, 177–78
Baret, Jeanne, 3–24, 157, 197
    childhood, 3–4
    contributions to science, 23

Baret, Jeanne (*cont.*)
   death, 23
   as housekeeper and assistant to
      Dr. Commerson, 5–8
   marriages, 21–22, 22–23
   on Mauritius, 21
   returns to France, 22
   sails around world, 10–21
   seeks to sail around world, 8–9
   in Tahiti, 16–19
Blackmores First Lady (boat), 155–56,
   167
   See also Cottee, Kay
Boddy, Brent, 181, 185
Bougainville, Admiral Louis-Antoine de,
   10, 15, 16, 17, 18, 19
Bunyoro (African kingdom), 33–34

Canada, Arctic, 79, 83–89
Cape Haze Marine Laboratory, Florida,
   125–29, 198
Carroll, Geoff, 181, 185
Casteret, Elisabeth, 97–111, 198
   birth of children, 102, 106, 107
   cave explorations, 97–100, 102–5,
      106–7
   death of, 108
   discovers cave paintings, 104–5
   meets and marries Norbert Casteret,
      98
   message on cave wall, 100, 110
   as mountain climber, 97
Casteret, Gilberte, 102–3, 105, 107, 108,
   109–10, 111
Casteret, Madame (Norbert's mother),
   97, 102, 104, 108
Casteret, Maud, 102, 107, 108, 109–10,
   111
Casteret, Norbert, 97–111
   searches for underground rivers,
      105
   takes children caving, 109–10
caving, *see* Casteret, Elisabeth

Chojnowska-Liskiewicz, Krystyna, 198–
   99
Clark, Eugenie, 126–28, 136–37, 198
Commerson, Dr. Philibert
   around-the-world voyage, 6–9, 12–19
   hires Jeanne Baret, 5
   illness and death, 20–21
   as naturalist, 5, 6–7
   son of, 5, 7, 20, 22, 23
Cook, Dr. Frederick, 75
Cottee, Kay, 153–67, 199
   achievements, 167, 199
   childhood interest in sailing, 153
   family and friends' support of, 154,
      155, 156
   first woman to complete solo nonstop
      voyage around world, 166, 199
   plans solo sail around world, 154–57
   sails alone around world, 157–66
Cross, Mrs. (cook), 57, 60, 63
Cumbre Ana Peck (Peruvian peak), 55

Dal Vera, Anne, 186, 187, 188, 194, 199
Diebitsch family, 56–58
dinosaurs, 170–74

Earle, Dr. Sylvia, 123–37, 198
   at Cape Haze Marine Laboratory,
      125–29
   childhood, 123–24
   first underwater dive, 124–25
   first woman NOAA chief scientist,
      136
   leads all-female aquanaut team, 129–
      31
   marriages and children, 125, 128,
      129–30, 133, 135, 136
   meets Eugenie Clark, 126–27
   sets solo dive record, 135, 198
   tests diving suit ("Jim"), 133, 135
   university studies, 125, 127, 129
   watches whales underwater, 131–33
Egingwah (Inuit man), 75

Egypt, 27–28, 39, 41, 137, 174
elephants, 136
Elgren, Tim, 177–179
Eskimos, *see* Inuit
Etoile (ship)
  leaves Jeanne Baret and Dr. Commerson in Mauritius, 21
  in Pacific, 16–19
  sails around South America, 14–16
  sets sail, 10, 12–13
  shipboard life, 13, 19–20
Everest, Mount, 140, 141–50

Field Museum of Natural History, 174
Fifth Thule Expedition, 96
fossils, hunting, 169–74

Gabriel (mountain guide), 50, 52–54
Giller, Sue, 186, 187, 188, 194, 199
Goddio, Franck, 173, 174
Grant, James, 29, 31, 40
Greenland
  Pearys in, 56–57, 58, 59, 60–65, 66, 67–75
  Rasmussen in, 78–83

Harper's Monthly Magazine, 49–50
Hawaii, 112, 131–32, 133, 135
Hendrickson, Sue, 168–76, 199
  discovers *T. rex* specimen, 171–72
  as diver, 168–69
  as fossil hunter, 169–74
  honored by University of Illinois, 176
  as marine archaeologist, 173–74
  searches for amber, 169–70
Henson, Matt, 62, 65, 68, 75
Himalayan Adventure Trust, 151
Himalayas, *see* Everest, Mount
Hirakawa, Hiroko, 140
Hisano, Eiko, 141, 142, 143, 144, 145, 146, 147
Huascarán, Mount, 45–55

Iggianguaq (Inuit man), 79, 80, 82
Inuit
  of Arctic Canada, 83–84, 85, 86
  of Alaska, 91–94
  in Greenland, 59, 60
  Josephine Peary aids, 69, 71–72
  as mothers, 57, 61, 91
  and Peary expeditions, 61, 63–64, 65, 75
  on Rasmussen expedition, 79–90
  See also Arnarulunguaq (Inuit woman)

Jeanne d'Arc, 3, 4, 8, 9–10, 22
Jivaro Indians, 120–21

Kamrasi (king of Bunyoro), 34
Koodluktoo (Inuit boy), 61–62, 64, 65, 69, 72, 73

Ladies Climbing Club of Japan, 140
Larson, Peter, 170–71, 172–73
Lee, Hugh, 65

Mantell, Bob, 181–82, 184
marine archaeology, *see* Hendrickson, Sue
marine biology, *see* Earle, Dr. Sylvia
Matterhorn, 44, 139
Mauritius, 20–22
Maxwell, Nicole, 112–22, 198
  as ballet dancer, 112, 116, 120
  becomes interested in healing plants, 114–15
  initial visit to Peru, 113–15
  marriage, 112–13
  searches Amazonian rain forest for healing plants, 116–22
McKerrow, Robert, 181, 182, 183
McKinley, Mount, 177–78
Miteq (Inuit man), 79, 80–81, 83, 84–91, 94, 95

mountain climbing, see Peck, Annie
    Smith; Tabei, Junko
Murchison, Sir Roderick, 39

National Geographic Society, 44, 76, 136
National Oceanic and Atmospheric
    Administration (NOAA), 136
Nerrivik (Inuit goddess), 77–78, 82, 83,
    95
Nile River
    Bakers' search for source, 26, 28–37
    sources of, 26, 31, 36–38, 41
North Pole, reaching, 75, 185, 197, 198

Ooqueah (Inuit man), 75
Ootah (Inuit man), 75

Pacific Ocean, 16, 159–60
paleontology, see Hendrickson, Sue
Payne, Katy, 131, 136, 198
Payne, Roger, 131, 136
Peary, Francine, 66–67, 73
Peary, Josephine Diebitsch, 56–76, 197
    aids Inuit families, 69, 71, 72
    birth of babies, 61, 66, 75
    death of second child, 67
    family, 56–58
    first white woman to cross Arctic
        Circle in Greenland, 58, 197
    in Greenland, 56–57, 58, 59–65, 66,
        67–75
    honored by National Geographic
        Society, 76
    icebound in Arctic, 69–73
    leaves Greenland for U.S., 65, 66, 75
    pregnancies, 57, 60, 66
    raises money for husband, 66
    sails for Greenland, 56, 58–60, 66, 67
    shipboard life, 67–68
Peary, Marie Ahnighito
    as advocate for father, 75–76
    birth, 61
    life in Greenland, 62, 64, 65, 68–75

life in U.S., 65–66, 67
Peary, Robert, 180, 197
    Arctic explorations, 58–61, 63, 64
    fathers Inuit child, 71
    quest to reach North Pole, 57, 58, 63–
        64, 65, 66, 73–74
    reaches North Pole, 75
    refuses to take Josephine on North
        Pole trek, 63–64, 65
    suffers frostbite, 67, 73–74
Peary, Robert, Jr., 75
Peck, Annie Smith, 42–55, 197–98
    in Alps, 43, 44
    childhood and education, 42–43
    climbs Matterhorn, 44
    climbs North American peaks, 44
    expeditions to climb Mount Huas-
        carán, 45–54
    first woman to reach top of previously
        unsummited mountain, 53, 55,
        198
    meets Teddy Roosevelt, 49
    peak named for, 54–55
    as teacher, 43
Peru
    Annie Smith Peck in, 45–49, 50, 52–
        55
    Nicole Maxwell in, 113–15, 116–22
    Sue Hendrickson in, 170
Pyrenees Mountains, 97–100

Quechua Indians, 46

rain forest, Amazonian
    Nicole Maxwell's searches for healing
        plants in, 114–22
Rasmussen, Knud, 77–96, 198
    in Greenland, 77–83
    records Inuit stories, 77–78, 79, 84,
        85–86
    return to Denmark, 94–95
    trek across Arctic Canada, 83–90
Roosevelt, Theodore, 49

Royal Geographical Society, 40–41, 113
Rudolf (mountain guide), 50, 52–54, 55
Rukas (Jivaro witch doctor), 120

Sahara Desert, 41
sailing, *see* Baret, Jeanne; Cottee, Kay
sangre de grado trees, 122
Schurke, Paul, 181, 183, 184, 185
Seeglo (Inuit man), 75
Shackleton, Ernest, 180, 190
sharks, 125, 126–27, 128, 129, 136–37
Sherpas, 140–42, 144–50
Society of Women Geographers, 55
Sorby, Sunniva, 186, 187, 188, 194, 199
South America, 14–16, 160
    Annie Smith Peck in, 45–49, 50, 52–
      55
    Nicole Maxwell in, 113–22
    See also Peru
South Dakota, 170–73
South Pole, reaching, 187, 188, 192
Speke, John, 29, 31, 40
Steger, Will, 178–80, 181, 183, 185
Sue (dinosaur), *see Tyrannosaurus rex*

Tabei, Junko, 138–52, 198
    achievements, 151–52, 198
    childhood, 138–39
    education, 139
    first woman to summit Mount Ever-
      est, 149–50, 198
    and Ladies Climbing Club of Japan,
      140
    marriage and children, 139, 140
    Mount Everest climb, 141–50
    summits Annapurna, 140
Tahiti, 16–19
Tektite II (undersea lab), 130–31
Tesa (Jivaro woman), 120–21
Tinné, Alexandrine, 29–30, 41, 197
Tinné, Madame (mother), 29–30

Tshering Sherpa, Ang, 142, 143, 144,
    146, 147, 149
Tyrannosaurus rex, 171–73, 174

Vanderbilt family, 126
Victoria, Lake, 31, 40, 41
Victoria, Queen, 31, 36, 38, 40
Vinatéa sisters, 45
Virgin Islands, 130–31

Weber, Richard, 181, 185
whales, 131–33
Windward (ship), 67–69
Witoto Indians, 116–18
women in exploration
    first non-native woman to cross Arctic
      Circle in Greenland, 58, 197
    first non-native woman to give birth
      north of Arctic Circle, 61
    first woman to reach a Nile River
      source, 37, 197
    first woman to reach North Pole on
      foot, 185, 198
    first woman to reach previously un-
      summited major peak, 55, 198
    first woman to sail around world, 22,
      197
    first woman to sail solo, nonstop,
      around world, 166, 198–99
    first woman to ski alone to South
      Pole, 190
    first woman to summit highest peaks
      on seven continents, 151
    first woman to summit Mount Ever-
      est, 149–50, 198
    first woman to trek to both poles,
      188
    first women to cross Antarctica on
      foot, 199
    first women to reach South Pole on
      skis, 199